Journey Planner

ROWAN B FORTUNE
(Editor)

Published by Cinnamon Press, Meirion House, Tanygrisiau, Blaenau Ffestiniog, Gwynedd LL41 3SU
www.cinnamonpress.com

ISBN 978-1-909077-16-4

British Library Cataloguing in Publication Data. A CIP record for this book can be obtained from the British Library.

Designed and typeset in Garamond & Palatino by Cinnamon Press.
Cover design by Jan Fortune fromoriginal artwork 'Londond Big Ben Silhouette' by Refugeek © Refugeek, agency dreamtime.

Cinnamon Press is represented by Inpress and by the Welsh Books Council in Wales.
Printed in Poland

Introduction

The episodic vignettes of Clare Fisher's winning 'Journey Planner: from wherever you are to Peckham' is almost a chain of prose poems that involves the reader with its future-tense second-person-perspective stream-of-consciousness; a snapshot gallery that jars between comic and tragic pictures of modernity through the life of its protagonist. Much of the prose of this collection is similarly avant-gardist in approach; like how Tracey Iceton plays a bleak double entendre with her narrative reworking of a catastrophe in 'Slag'.

The poets, also, jettison expectations. David Wilson inspects his subject matter sideways, whether his content be the first person pronoun or love; so 'In Praise of Sleet' he elevates this inconsequence, 'no grand plan for transfiguration/ won't stop retreats from Moscow/ or you reaching Tesco.' and invisibility, 'It slips away while Brueghel mixes paint.' Kathleen M. Quinlan also draws on meteorological inspiration for 'Journeying through Fog' in which the sound patterns of the opening bear an onomatopoeic relation to the subject and the poem wears its devices on its sleeve, 'The paddles crack the silence / with rhythmic plunk and plash,'

The winning poet, David Olsen, is concerned with liminal states 'between sleep and waking,/ where identity is lost' and the intersections of phenomenology and history 'non-Euclidean vanishing point// beneath an iron gateway/ to the new millennial truth:/ ARBEIT MACHT FREI' It is as if he is engaged in the task of recovering lifeworlds, 'Wyeth's tempera palette is equally quiet/ and lacking plot; context is all.' And in that connection of subjectivity and time he is able to cleverly collapse distinctions and juxtapose, '1950s. Duck-and-cover.[…] 2010s. Lockdown.'

Rowan B. Fortune
Tŷ Meirion, January, 2014

Contents

Journey Planner

Journey Planner:
from wherever you are to Peckham
Clare Fisher

1. Journey time: *30 minutes*

When walking from the St Pancras International East Midlands Mainline to the Underground, stop and scratch your foot outside your girlfriend's favourite shops: Oliver Bonas, Cath Kidson, Foyles. Point out the narrow shelf of sale items at the back. Remind her that her second favourite sister's birthday is coming up.

Lead her back to the East Midlands Mainline platform by mistake. Ask, is she's sure she doesn't want to go back to Derby. Laugh like you've just made a really funny joke; stare at her until she works out that this is the opposite of a joke, that all you want to do is rattle away from this city that cocoons that time back in the dark ages of your childhood that you never tell anyone about not even yourself you don't want people thinking you're weird.

When she tells you to stop being silly, squeeze her hand until everything that is inside of you seeps into her; when she feels that dark, sticky stuff slip through her veins, she, too, will want to go home.

2. Journey Time: *43 minutes*

Pretend you're someone else; someone who has never been to Peckham before, someone who cannot believe it has no tube and only one weird little train; someone who cannot stop oohing at every late-opening hairdresser and grocery selling fruits of ponderable exotic names and pun-heavy fried chicken joint. Someone who has worked his way through the six pack that he bought in the *M&S Simply Food* way back at King's Cross. Someone who makes your girlfriend squint, as if she can't quite see you.

By the time you make the journey in reverse the next afternoon, you will not know why your girlfriend's mates think you're an idiot (the guys)/crazy (the girls). You will not know why your girlfriend is more intent on reading the *Sports* section of a grubby *Torygraph* she found on the floor, than talking to you; you would like to ask her what she's done with your other normal girlfriend who comes out in a rash upon hearing the word *sport*, but the only thing that you now know about life is this clang-bang-bang in your head.

In the months to come, when you are sloshing through the soggy Peak District green, and she says, 'Hey, do you remember that night you went mental in London? Do you remember how you tried to get my friend to take off her *I heart Peckham* t-shirt and how, when she did, you said that you wanted to jizz in it and that she had nice tits?'

You stop. You wipe the rain drops off your glasses so that you can see into each other's eyes.

You say, 'No.'

3. Journey Time: *information unavailable*

You could just tell her. You could open your mouth as you push your way onto the train and press it right up against her small round ear. You could leave it there until the whole thing was out there for her and any eavesdroppers to know; you could stay on the Victoria Line until it terminates in Brixton and a pre-recorded posh lady's voice tells you to hop off.

She could hold your head and tell you that it wasn't your fault, that you're going to Peckham to meet her oldest, bestest friends; all you have to do is snap the thin thread of anxiety stringing the now-you to the past.

You could cry into her lap. You could ride the tube and the train and the bus until all the tears and the words were out. When you step onto the Peckham concrete you'd fly, you'd be so pure and so light. You could go into her friend's house and shake their hands and offer intelligent opinions on intelligent subjects and even flash them little bits of your soul. You could hold this up as the first night that you became a part of each other's past-worlds. You would never have to hold anything back from her again, because if she could know that about you and still love you and still love you and still love you, she still loves you no matter what.

Attention: there are important engineering works being carried out on this line, the major engine of which is your mouth; no one knows when they might end (not even TFL).

4. Journey Time: *years*

Leg One

When a spare room in your girlfriend's friends' house becomes free at the same time as you get that dreaming skyscraper job, move in. Cover the walls with smudgy photos of your just-finished life that you printed out on your Mum's computer; make sure to leave space for beer mats, gig tickets, posters, flyers, leaflets and free magazine covers that you steal/keep every time you live a bit more of this new one.

Mind the gaps between work and *Lidl* and sleep, between *Peep Show* replays and joints and beers, between parties and pubs and long queues in the cold for disappointing (but you don't like to admit it) warehouse club nights. If you feel you might fall in, grab your girlfriend, tight.

Leg Two

When your lease is up and your friends are moving north/south/abroad and your thirtieth birthday is staring you in the face and you are now paid enough to never say yes to a receipt when you take out cash, and you and your girlfriend talk about getting a deposit on a flat, and she says that in fact she's already found the perfect place, just around the corner from where you are now, not much bigger than a corner itself but still, it's cool, it's the kitchen of an old brewery, or maybe the toilet, say: yes.

Transfer time

Look out of the window of your new/old brewery toilet/flat and see the library and remember how you and your girlfriends and your friends would make it down there at about five on a Sunday afternoon and someone would always joke that they should go and study and every else would laugh and then cross the street to *Noodles Noodles All You Can Eat,* which was only going to deepen your hangover, but where you still stuffed your face in some sort of misguided preparation for the coming week.

Leg Three

Take your girlfriend to the coffee shops you would never go to with your friends; put your hand on top of hers as you try to read the paper over the toddlers' screams. Go with her to galleries and pop-up cinema showings. But accept that with just the two of you, the silence to people ratio has tipped; tip it further by crying quietly in your sleep, and when she asks what's wrong, say does she think it's time for a baby. Don't be scared when she replies, I was hoping you were going to say that.

Final Leg

And it is exactly eleven months later, when you are delirious from lack of sleep, when the past and the present and the future and the what-ifs are pressing down on you in one damp screaming muddle, that you say, 'you know my Dad used to live here.'

'Sssh,' she says, 'She's just gone to sleep.'

Two days later, as you both stare into the silence that is now a blessing so rare and so precious that neither of you know what to do with it, she turns to you, and says, 'What was that you were saying about your Dad?'

'Just that he used to live in Peckham.' You don't dare say more, not now, with the dull afternoon light pouring through the new/old brewery/toilet window.

'Right,' she says, and for the first time since you moved in, she smiles at you like you're a puzzle she's still trying to figure out.

'I thought you didn't know your Dad,' she says, as one Saturday morning you are pushing the pram round the Rye.

'I didn't,' you say, staring hard at the crows that pick, pick, pick at the soggy ground.

'But you said…'

'He grew up here. He moved back after my Mum kicked him out. I missed him and I missed him. Eventually she let me stay. He took me to a football match. He let me wear one of his shirts and his friends gave me sips of beer. But on the tube home, they crowded round this man. Telling him to *go home, go home, go home*. I remember thinking it was strange; they didn't even know him. How could they know where was his home? Didn't even occur to me it had anything to do with him being black. They followed him off the train. I followed. I followed them to the edge of this park. I watched them beat him up until he could no longer move. Right there.'

You point to the other side of the muddy grass, where a chubby teenage girl with a lolly in her mouth is teaching a tiny boy with wild hair to ride a bike. You steer the pram off the path and over the grass; when the wheels crush the grass on the spot, you stop.

The boy is saying he can't do it, he can't do it, and the girl is saying something that is garbled by the lolly.

'Afterwards, he acted like nothing happened. He took me to MacDonalds. I acted like nothing happened, too, except that I couldn't eat my chicken nuggets, and he got really mad. I ate them then threw up. Then he took me back to Kings Cross and I got the train home and I never told my Mum or anyone else what happened, just that I didn't want to see him not ever again.'

'Watch out!' She grabs your arm; your hands grip the pram and the three (four?) of you tumble back just in time to see the boy and his hair whizz past screaming, *don't let go!*

You watch his little legs push the peddles that turn the wheels until they get stuck in the mud and the bike stops and he falls off and the girl runs over to him at a speed that you find remarkably fast. The lolly stick somersaults over her shoulder.

'Riding was fun,' says the boy, 'But falling off was funner.'

'You retard,' she says.

They both laugh.

'Fucking hell,' says your girlfriend.

Watch the lolly stick sink into the mud. Look up at the sky. Breathe in these strangers' voices that rush past your ears. Feel the roughness of your girlfriend's February-frozen palm on the back of your hand and know that you are here.

David Wilson

Advice on 'I love you'

Mariko, please be aware that,
as with *Watashi, Ore, Atashi,*
there are many different
characters for the pronoun 'I'.

It might be the id, or ego,
the lyric 'I', or an 'I' later
disowned as drunk, divided,
or still to find itself.

Perhaps better simply to say 'love',
a state without subject or object,
like the opening cherry blossom
in your classic poem with no title.

'I love you'

My parents didn't use this phrase,
talked in terms of work to do, and weather
and how they were bringing us up;
despite whispered rows at night
stayed together, held in place by good form.
They were not much given to using 'I'.

Near the end, my father asked a nurse
to bring my waiting mother
to the side-room of his suffering,
having taken ten minutes to stand up
straight, always the military man,
nearly losing his balance.

One has to be brave at a time like this,
he said, taking her hand,
Some things must be done alone.
And then, *Thank you for loving me.*
A slight bow and turn, while she cried
in the voice of a young girl
'Oh my darling'.

In Praise of Sleet

Artist of the passing moment,
it floats, falls, dissolves;
isn't deep; doesn't accumulate,
impose a blank year-zero page.
Wouldn't dream of making a scene.

It has no grand plan for transfiguration
won't stop retreats from Moscow
or you reaching Tesco.
Doesn't want you to lie down and be an angel;
leaves Furey's grave untouched.

Doesn't have fifty names for itself;
no need to fret if it fails to arrive,
to think of fractured Arctic shelves
and polar bears trapped on floes
like double mattresses cast adrift.

It won't haunt you with a melting story
about how you should have left more tracks
in December in Minnesota, or called across
a glittering slope to Marie, 'hold on tight'.
It slips away while Brueghel mixes paint.

Night in the Borders

Lying on my back, alone in bed,
at three and four o'clock,
occasional trucks the only sound,
I think of you alone.

A hiss of tyres on wet road
from the left ear to the right,
the pause and hum of higher gears,
a howl that fades along the straight.

Do you, also, imagine the drivers,
their music, what they carry,
darkness tunnelled in front of them,
rolling in again behind?

Bethany Rivers

Lost

Every map in the world
blackened with raging fire
Every sat' nav' melted.

Every compass and telescope broken,
stamped on, trampled and crumpled
by hammer and chisel and booted foot.

There are no edges anymore
all the boundaries are gone:
there's no mine, no yours.

All the countries have lost their names,
forests grow in the seas
houses stuck in the desert.

The world is flat again
the land all one and the waves
are remote tear drops

we used to cry.
There is no left or right.
There is no north or south.

Phil Madden

Susurro

'El susurro del aire…entre magnolios, limoneros'- Luis Cerruda , 1920—
Seville

Of course he knew
Guernica would come.
Just not the name.
Just not the shape.
And the clockwork gorriones
would have harried up his rhythm.

But still…
Susurro.Susurro.Susurro.

Lime Yellow Fleeting

pounding

your path

sounding

off about your heart

without sounding

out if I wanted to know

not straying

we passed

a nuthatch

fieldfares

the lime yellow fleeting

of a green woodpecker

buzzard

ravens

you did not

see them

there was not

even a 'what

was th..?'

they just

passed you by

until we came to the end.

There Are No Tame Words

He grew the all year round variety.
Hardy. Prolific.
Was generous with them.
Gave some to whoever he met.

He kept them in a cage.
They fed well. Bred well.
They knew every word that he said, he said.

He was found in the garden.
The brassica razor red.
The hamsters asleep in his throat.
He understood nothing we said, they said.

Vermin

Rosemary Mairs

The intensity of her grief will pass. She tells herself this; she knows this, she should do at her age, but it doesn't make it easier.

Philip isn't grieving; he isn't even pretending. She knows he had only pretended to like Maisie May. He'd made a fuss from the moment she arrived, when he came home from work one evening and the new arrival was in a basket in the kitchen, a tiny whisp of ginger fluff.

'It's only because of my asthma,' he had said. 'If it wasn't for that…'

Then a big deal was made of everything, even something simple like a cat flap, saying that mice would get in, could she not let the cat out the door instead.

The cat.

They had married just a few years ago; she had thought him a kind, thoughtful man, a companion for her later years, but she saw a different side to him after Maisie May arrived. He hadn't gone with her to the vet's for Maisie May's inoculations, or to the pet store for all the things she needed, didn't admire the new pink velvet collar with the cute little bell.

Instead, he tried to make out that his chest was worse. He even went to the doctor; cat hair was the worst for someone like him he had supposedly been told, more so than that of a dog.

She began hoovering the house more often so he had no excuse to complain, was already hoovering as he left for work, again after dinner, again as he watched the ten o'clock news. He started walking, every night, even in the rain, even in the cold. No wonder he had a bad chest.

Now that Maisie May is gone, he sits in front of the TV again, never ventures out in the evening, even though it is summertime, even though it is perfect walking weather.

'There's kittens in the paper,' she says, and she knows immediately from his face that she was right to suspect him. 'Free to a good home. One might be lonely on its own. I think I'll get two.'

He puts his hand inside his jacket pocket where he keeps his inhaler, as if the very thought of two cats in the house will give him an asthma attack. The only way he could redeem himself now would be to say: *But it's too soon after Maisie May.* If he was clever he would say that. But he isn't clever; he has only been promoted once in his thirty-five years with Prentice Printers.

'I… I didn't,' he stammers, 'I didn't think you'd want another one.'

He knew if he got rid of Maisie May she wouldn't be replaced.

'Maybe you're right,' she says, even smiling at him. 'And at least we'll be able to go on holiday now,' she adds, just to see his reaction, and his mouth drops open, 'You… you want to…'

It was two years since they'd gone away, the summer before she'd got Maisie May they'd gone to Blackpool. He had wanted to put Maisie May in a cattery so they could go to Cornwall the following year.

A cattery.

She goes for a walk; she can't bear to be in the house with him, never mind go on holiday. When she reaches the main road she turns right, her fingers fiddling with the collar in her pocket, listening to the muffled chime of the tiny bell.

It *was* him. Who else would want to harm Maisie May? 'Poisoning.' She'll never forget the vet saying it.

'Ethylene glycol… anti-freeze,' the vet had continued, 'in the stomach contents.'

'Wh-what… what do you mean?' She could hardly get the words out.

'It has a very sweet taste, cats like it,' the vet went on.

'You- you mean… *on purpose?*'

'Not everyone's a cat lover I'm afraid.'

She had told Philip that evening, everything the vet had said, intently watching his face for signs of guilt.

'Maybe he means pigeon keepers,' he finally said.

She had stared at him with incomprehension.

'When the vet said not everyone's a cat lover. It's common knowledge that pigeon keepers hate cats.'

She has walked further than she intended, and she has already been up and down this road several times before, looking for a pigeon shed in someone's garden, for any sign of birds.

Her fingers clasp tighter the velvet collar in her pocket. There are no pigeon keepers; she has been around the whole area. It *must* have been Philip. Who else wanted rid of her?

No one. Just Philip. Just her husband. She feels overcome at the realisation that it was definitely him, putting out a hand to steady herself, holding onto the garden fence beside her. How easy it must have been, to take the anti-freeze from the garage shelf, to pour it into a saucer.

'Can I help you?'

A man walks down the driveway towards her; he must think she's loitering outside his house.

She pulls herself together, letting go of the fence.

'Are you okay?'

He's young; half her age. She isn't used to being treated courteously by the younger generation, more used to being pushed past in the supermarket, ignored by them in queues.

She smiles at him. 'I'm fine, thank you.' As she begins to walk away, she pauses, turning. 'Actually, I wonder if you could tell me. Is there… are there, any pigeon keepers around here?'

He looks at her strangely, and she knows it was an odd question to ask. 'Why?' he says. 'Why do you want to know?'

She flounders for a moment, trying to think of a reply. 'It's just… I like them… I like pigeons.'

He shakes his head. 'No one round here, far as I know. But we only moved in a few months back.'

She nods, turning, walking quickly on. She had actually said it —*I like pigeons*. Pigeon keepers liked pigeons, people who were capable of poisoning other people's beloved cats… people like her husband.

The first time she does it, it's unintentional. Philip takes tablets each morning. They are already in a box with compartments for each day of the week, and she tips them into an egg cup. But today she accidentally spills them onto the bench, because she's upset, anyone in her situation would be, not concentrating on what she is doing. She scoops them up and puts them in the egg cup, four tablets… no, wait, there's just three. She looks on the bench, on the floor, to no avail… She waits for him to notice at breakfast that one isn't there, but he tips them into his mouth and washes them down with tea as usual.

He comes home that evening with a travel guide to Cornwall, saying that he slipped out to get it in his lunch break.

'Did you have a good day? How was your chest?' she asks.

He smiles, yes, his day was fine and so was he, obviously pleased that she cares about his well-being.

Again, the second time, it's not intentional, not really. She is looking at the vitamin tablets she got a while back and never took. They're very similar, she thinks, to one of Philip's four. She swaps them over in the egg cup, you really couldn't tell the difference, and then Philip is behind her, carrying the tray with the breakfast things over to the table, before she can swap them back.

Again, no reaction, and there wouldn't have been a third time if he hadn't done it. She couldn't understand it; Maisie May's basket was gone from the corner of the kitchen. It had been there the night before; she always looked at it before going up to bed, blinking back a tear, picturing her darling curled up inside. She found it in the garage, beside the bin, and she knew he'd almost put it in the bin, but then thought better of it.

She doesn't mean to continue, but she can't seem to stop herself; she owes it to Maisie May. She keeps picturing him filling a saucer in the garage, watching it being lapped up. And anyway, he mustn't need them, his health issues are obviously exaggerated just to get sympathy—Poor Philip and his bad chest.

The phone call one day surprises her. Her husband taken from the office to hospital with palpitations after an asthma attack.

He looks pale and drained at visiting time and she berates herself; how could she have done it? He has to take off his oxygen mask to speak, telling her not to worry; he puts it back over his mouth, closing his eyes as if it was such an effort to talk to her.

When the phone rings the following day she knows it will be the hospital. Her heart flutters, but he's back on his proper medication again, he'll be fine, she tries to convince herself. They are ringing to tell her that he has picked up an infection. He can't have visitors; they'll keep her informed. 'But he has a weak chest…' she says, panic rising in her voice, and they calmly repeat that they'll keep her informed.

As soon as she sets down the phone, it rings again.

It's a man this time, and when he tells her who he is she reaches out a hand out to steady herself, gripping the back of a kitchen chair. But she hadn't meant him any real harm.

'I believe your cat died,' the policeman says.

She can't speak. She'd been so sure he was going to ask her about Philip's tablets.

He explains that he's been contacted by her vet.

She has to pull herself together.

'Your cat was poisoned by anti-freeze?' he asks, to confirm this was the cause. 'There have been similar incidents recently in your area. We're following a line of enquiry. We'll keep you informed.'

She goes outside, walking blindly to the main road; a van toots at her, and she realises that she had stepped off the pavement. How could she have done it? But it's only an infection… people pick up infections all the time in hospital. But she knew what would happen; she knew what she had done. It would go into his chest. His weak chest.

She is dizzy, but there's nothing to grab hold of to steady herself; she can see a fence ahead, recognising it is the one she held onto last time. She makes herself breathe deeply, waiting for the light-headedness to pass.

It's then that she hears it, but it must be in her mind, because that was what she was listening for last time she walked this far—cooing.

There it is again, and she walks slowly forward, until she reaches the garden fence, then up the driveway and along the side of the house; it is as if the birds are calling her in. There's a large shed, and she can smell them now, the way a cat would; drawing it in.

'Can I help you?' A young woman with a toddler on her hip, wary of this stranger in her back yard.

She has to think quickly. 'Your husband… I… I was talking to your husband…' She indicates to the shed. 'I like them… pigeons that is.'

The young woman smiles. 'They only come this week.'

She nods, smiling back. 'But you've been here a few months?'

The young woman shifts the toddler onto her other hip. 'Gary didn't want to bring them 'til now. You got any?' she asks.

'No,' she shakes her head. 'No, there's too many cats where I live.'

The young woman nods. 'I like cats, me, but some chance us gettin' one,' She looks over to the shed. 'Gary says they're vermin.'

The phone is ringing when she gets back home, but she doesn't answer it. She can't think about Philip just now. She will later, but not just now.

She had liked him, Gary, that day at his house, for asking if she was okay. *Gary says they're vermin.*

She doesn't do it intentionally, it's not as if she purposely waits until dark; it's not as if she plans it. She lies in bed with the curtains open, thinking—it's a bright night, the moon will light the way, and she gets up, gets dressed, and goes downstairs.

She carries what she needs with her. The birds are startled by her presence, begin kicking up a racket, so she has to be quick before Gary appears; he's probably already jumping out of bed, thinking, *I bet it's another bastard cat*, and she waits only until she's sure it's properly caught, and the flames are racing up towards the moon. The birds are shrieking now, screaming for Gary to save them as she walks back down the driveway.

When she gets home she sits at the kitchen table until daylight, and then she phones the hospital. Philip's condition has improved slightly; he's responding to the antibiotics. They can pass on a message for her to her husband.

'Tell him…' She almost says, 'Tell him I'm sorry,' before clearing her throat. 'Cornwall… Tell him, Cornwall,' and she hangs up.

She goes over to the corner of the kitchen, picks up Maisie May's basket, taking it out to the garage, putting it beside the bin, and then after taking a deep breath, puts it into the bin.

Back in the house, she packs some of his underwear and another pair of Philip's pyjamas to leave for him at the hospital. She wonders if Gary is there, his hands and arms burnt—she feels regret for a moment, but then she pictures him pouring the anti-freeze, and her remorse shrivels away.

The Cornwall brochure is in the magazine rack, and she puts it into the bag with the pyjamas. She's not one for holidays, she hadn't really enjoyed Blackpool, but she knows that she owes it to Philip. She has put on her coat when the doorbell rings; through the window she can see the bright blue and yellow lines of a police car.

Maybe, they will take her to the hospital to leave Philip's things on the way to the station; she wants him to see that she's made the effort, especially bringing the brochure.

Through the front door's frosted glass she gazes at the uniformed silhouettes at the other side. She straightens her shoulders, ready to explain about last night, to answer questions; she can even show them the paraffin canister and matches in the garage where she left them,

'Vermin,' she will say. 'I was just getting rid of vermin.'

Joan Lennon

Anniversary

I slid past your first deathday
thinking of herring

how there in the shoal
you wore your silver
with a difference
your flick and shimmer
always
only
yours

how we still swirl on

how the ocean is not the same

Her Dementia—Those Last Years

Pale boats navigate
the silted beds of old rivers,
lose their way,
meander into fields of corn
where sand soil shows
like scalp, and

the settlement
round the next bend,
gnawed by rust and woodworm,
has forgotten the sound
each boat's unique whistle used to make,
remembrance clogged,

drowned
out, by
the drumming of termites,
the hammer of brown rain
on corrugated tin,
runnels leading nowhere

Heidi James-Dunbar

Paradise Found

(For Delaine Le Bas)

Listen.
They are listening.
Do you hear them? I found it. It was lost. But now it is mine. They see, there are eyes everywhere. They see and are afraid. A flock of magpies, dandy in their black and whites, follow me. From the rooftops the birds descend in random numbers and from this I deduce my future. A retinue is it? Yes, a retinue. They attend me. Today seven wait on the window ledge pecking impatiently at the glass and each other's feet. I feed them crumbs of bread and pork rind. Seven is my lucky number. I am cold, I burn books to stay warm, the pages curl like black roses. I see Jesus, blood in his hair, on his face, his body, his long thighs, he is cast in a red glow. I kiss his feet, it is required. This room is cold.

I sit and sew. My hands, bone white, ink splashed, delicate, long nails encrusted with bright colours. My hands, precise like a jeweller. The threads pierce and contain. I love, my love never falters. I sit in the shadow of my own flesh. There is a message being tapped out on the wall, they want me out. They say 'you do not belong, with your pig children, your red hair, and clever hands.' They want me out; they try to smoke us out, like vermin. The flames of their fire prod and tear at the dark. I am not afraid. The children squeal. They will learn. They have to.

The horses wait, their proud flesh, hot and foam flecked, as if immerging from water. They do not speak, cannot speak, with only limbs to escape. Language eludes, evades them. They are immersed. There are messages hidden in their mouths. They speak to me and only me. A contradiction, but I do not lie. Truth is in movement. My ancestor's legacy is me. I am the bequeathed and the horses know this. We travel together through mute terrain; our language is not shared with the outsiders. The outsiders face their walls, which move closer and closer as time penetrates the flesh. I am, I am. I wear a necklace of butterfly cocoons, they rattle in anticipation, I wait for their colours. The horses wear their ropes but do not need them. We are bound in blood, with Christ, each other. Let me tell you something. They are watching. Eyes everywhere. Let me tell you something. They stone us, throw rocks at our heads, at our children; and while doing it they hold balloons, blow whistles, it's a carnival, a festival of violence. I've seen them, I know them, once I saw a policeman box the ears of a kid because it threw stones at a cat 'Don't be cruel' he said. 'Don't be cruel to animals.' I see them as they see me. I am colour, light. I am shape and form. Everything that exists is an occurrence of light.

extracts from Pearl Lamb

I

Atomic Tsunami

Wash as slow as salt,
The lunar gather and retreat, gather and retreat,
Collects in severe points
Forming fragile rocks,
Future wounds concealed in the
Sharp edges.
It breaks down slow as sand
Progress of reduction and collection,
Reformation. Circling.
A process halted by speed.
As critical as metal
A judgment formed of action.
Tender erosion has no place here
Outgrown by new machines, waves, wind
A tree planted last year grows
Too slow to see
But grows
Too slow.
Sickle-shaped, light is
Swallowed by its heavy dark,
As the water collapses.
The sharp trajectory of light
Forced into unnatural corners
Recorded, new old screams echo
In Tantalite chambers. Days yet, they are more fragile than primal
Handprints on rock walls.
Forgotten, but watched over and over,
A repeated forgetting, in two dimensions.
Seafarers still, we float
Rules maintain our position,
Laws that even raw
Belief can't touch.
It is the scatter of fragments

That is hoped for now
Sifted through, a silt of
Domesticated terrors.
As data bolts, spooks then settles
Like glass, revealing cherished privacies.
We rebuild fences, willful, eyes closed,
Let machines remember.

III
Hands

a pan of water distinguishes
the treasure from the dirt
that traditional hands pull and wash
tip filter and collect
for shiny specks of cosmic substance
that allow fresh theatrics in improved colonies
bent double old practices unearth new
valuables
whole economies of affect and desire
reside in the suck
of infants strapped to mothers
backs
growing and growing
bug-eyed
they learn by watching
and want comes in
technological hungers are more easily
fixed
than resisting hands cut off at the wrist and
slung into the forest

A Night at Arlington Villas

Joanna Campbell

Mark wished he could lick a tissue like his mother used to when he was small. She would dash her tongue over it and stroke his grimy mouth or grazed knees, as if cleaning fish, but close to a kiss.

He wanted to kiss away the shiny blue colour on Tania's eyelids. They glinted like bruised almonds as she flicked the pages of a magazine in the darkening carriage. He wanted to warm them with his tongue, melt away the blue until her veins seeped their green ink through the skin.

Her hair was different too, the ends teased up with a hot brush at Janice's house just before she came to the station. And he didn't know her patent bag. The late sun on the platform had glared on it, hurting his eyes.

He stood up and lifted it onto the rack above Tania's head. She crossed her legs, the suspended foot rotating as he pushed the bag back. But she didn't look up at him.

'You look like you're always doing this,' he said, frowning.

'I don't,' she said, crushing the corner of the horoscope page between her finger and thumb.

'Don't look like it or don't always do this?'

Tania sighed. She uncrossed her thighs and they slurped apart, damp from the heat.

Mark hadn't seen her smile since their fingers laced on the platform. The sunlight had filtered through his shirt and the air smelt of holidays. Their bags had slumped on the ground, not neat like suitcases, but childish with bulges and hollows. A yellow slip lolled out of hers. His trainers were in a plastic bag underneath his pyjamas. They might walk into the country when they arrived.

'Have you got shoes you can walk in?'

'Not really. But we'll be in the guest house the whole time anyway.'

He looked at her sandals, the cork wedge as thick as a sandwich, the slender black straps snaking like liquorice laces around her ankles.

'They look like Janice Harvey's shoes.'

'They *are* Janice Harvey's.'

Tania looked up from the mangled magazine. As she caught his eye, laughter ruptured their silence, as it did in Chemistry two hours ago. No reason other than their secret, like a hidden slice of watermelon grinning in the fridge on a hot day.

It would be all right again now. His stomach buckled like gleeful chops under the grill.

She turned the pages back again and surveyed each one as if she had never seen it before, her eyebrows, plucked to black running-stitch, arching in surprise.

He took out a bag of Imperial Mints. 'Want one, Tan?'

'Not really.'

He wished he owned a sports jacket. But the next best thing was that he'd whipped the unpicking tool from the sewing basket under the hall table. After school he had waited until he rounded the corner into Standish Street and stitch-ripped the badge off the breast pocket of his blazer. On the train he was a grown man. And at Arlington Villas he would be an adult. Jacket and trousers. A few hairs bustling on his chin. No badge.

And Tania had the look of a wife. Her breasts were meaty-looking in a smocked blouse. Her fingers clanked with rings. She always kept them in a sock in her pocket until the final bell, then threaded them on until her hands were armour-plated. At Arlington Villas they would assume a wedding-band huddled among them.

Mark sucked on a mint, still straining towards Tania.

'Sit back, Mark. You're like a Jack Russell on a leash.'

She stroked her skirt with irritation as if he'd salivated and left a dollop. The shiny material clung like skin. He watched her wriggle to adjust it. He could only see the points of her knees now. Soon it would ride up to her thighs, splayed on the crusty velour of the seat.

He sat back, hands clasped behind his head, the sweet rattling on his back teeth.

The mint reminded him of the car-smell on days out when his Dad still had work and a licence and his breath wasn't thick with sour malt. Mark's mother always put Mark to bed early the night before.

'I must cut the sandwiches. Early start in the morning,' she'd say; her breath swift with excitement.

Mark would lie in his bed listening to the birds serenade the end of the day and his mother's knife slicing tomatoes and paring cheese. And his father would unfold crackling maps and make notes, his pencil scratching away beside the tomatoes.

Mark's mother always wore a white cardigan and set her hair on smaller curlers for the drive. He always sat behind her in the car, watching the marshmallow skin on the back of her neck, more pillowy than her tired face and creased eyes.

The back of his home shuddered past the train window. They all looked the same in his terrace. But he could pick his out because of the black pram by the coal bunker. It was nearly six, he reckoned. His mother would be slipping out any second now to lift his brother for the evening feed.

In this heat she dragged a kitchen chair out into the air and draped a towel over her chest like a man at the barber's. If the neighbours looked across from their washing-lines, the shroud made her feel less exposed. She preferred to keep to herself while they thrust open their back-doors to let out the smell of batter frying or the blare of their television or the tension of a quarrel. While pegs clattered into baskets and cardboardy doors slammed shut in the smallest breeze, the baby's beach-ball head swelled beneath the towel and its fish-mouth made smacking sounds in the still garden.

Mark preferred his mother to unfasten her blouse beside him on the settee while they watched television. He could smell her talcum powder, see a smudged line of it clinging to the sweat in the dip between her breasts. They strained with milk, the veins bruised from its pressure. The baby slept too soundly, letting the milk mount up as if were simmering and frothing in a pan on the gas. Sometimes it boiled over. His mother stuffed the tissues from under her cardigan cuff inside her slip to catch the leaks.

He always picked his brother up and passed him to her, feeling him shiver with hope, frantic lips searching, one hand resting like a starfish by the big smeary nipple, mouth gripping with relief.

Mark's shirt was clinging to his back. The seat prickled. He wished storms could wash the stiff air.

If rain soaked him and Tania, they could squelch upstairs to their room in Arlington Villas and steam by the heater, laughing at the downpour on the window of the darkening room. They could watch raindrops racing to the sill, like he did as a child.

And she would squeal at the lightning bolts. Grasp his arm as the thunder cracked through the sky and shook the walls. He would stroke her damp hair, usually sprayed into hard wings that stood crisp at each side of her head, but now rain-softened into tendrils. He would soothe her fear with kisses.

He waited for the dry brick rows and corrugated-iron roofs to sink behind hills, for the lines of baked clothes to disappear. He watched out for the fish-paste factory. Afterwards a few fields whisked by in a patchwork of parched sandy squares. A farm came and went. Then nothing much until grimy houses and flat industrial tracts passed the window.

'Thought Gloucester was the country,' Tania said.

'Well we're not there yet, are we?'

'Train's stopping, look. It says Gloucester.'

Mark had lost count of the stations.

The platform rose up. Roasting commuters out of their jackets and desperate for a cold drink at home peeled back cuffs and tugged at ties, their dark glasses reflecting the yellow train doors. They stared at the passengers inside the train, willing them to climb out.

Arlington Villas was three minutes' walk, sandwiched between a shuttered wool shop and a butcher finished for the day, his empty meat trays stained with traces of warm blood.

Mark had booked the room from an advert in his mother's magazine. *Delightful guest house*, it said, *in the very heart of Gloucester.*

Not far. Far enough. A room for them to be a couple in, he'd told Tania. She'd said a few times that she wanted him to be more of a man. This outing would prove it to her.

He'd booked it in the telephone-box by the Babylonia kebab-house. He'd lit a cigarette-end taken from the glass ashtray at home and deepened his voice to make the call. But the first number he dialled was wrong and the cigarette had gone out by the time he tried again. He managed the deep voice again, but felt a faint disappointment once the booking was made. It took no time and the receptionist at the delightful guest-house in the heart of Gloucester had barely said goodbye to him, hanging up without grace. As he stood in the box with the unused coppers being flung back out at him, he felt sick from the tobacco and the stench of the pressed meat and onions.

In the guest-house, they'd have cups of tea with saucers on a tray with a cloth. And a gong would announce dinner. That's how things were done. Tania would open her sooty eyes wide and look at him in a different way at Arlington Villas.

She had squeaked at the picture in the magazine of the floral eiderdown and humped-up pillows. She'd phoned Janice Harvey to tell her all about it. Mark wished she hadn't. But Tania had to say she'd be stopping over with Janice the night of Arlington Villas. Her Mum would wonder otherwise.

Mark's mother wouldn't ask questions if he stayed out. She and the baby went to bed tired at nine. She let the cocoa Mark made for her grow a skin. She snatched at sleep before the front door banged back against the wall, her night ruptured into fragments. Dad's knuckles at her mouth. His knee to her soft stomach.

Mark's room trembled from the iron bedstead thrashing against it from their side. Or sometimes her head.

Arlington Villas was a terraced house much like Mark's own. Their place was ground floor by the boiler room, they were told. Mark had planned his stance at the reception desk. Legs wide apart, one hand jingling Imperial Mints in his pocket. He twiddled a pair of sunglasses in his other hand, occasionally nibbling on the curved plastic arm. But the woman at Reception was busy snapping at a man in overalls who couldn't mend a cracked basin. She tossed Mark the key and her finger jabbed at the dark corridor that led them to a stifling room that smelt like the school caretaker's cubbyhole

'Hot isn't it?' Tania said, sitting on the bed. She poked at the brown quilt, finding a small tear that leaked feathers.

Mark fingered the Venetian blinds, trying to shift the bars of sun slicing through the slats. He pulled and twisted the grubby string, but blinding light still pierced the room, striping the thin carpet and gathering clouds of dust that hung in the mid-air.

'I'm starving,' Tania said. 'When's this dinner-gong going off then?'

While they waited, Mark did their chemistry homework and Tania repainted her nails. He unwrapped his bar of soap from Woolworth and put it in the saucer by the basin. No gong chimed.

'I'm missing my Mum's fritters tonight for this,' Tania said. Her voice had lost its bounce, so it couldn't even sound angry with him now. The sun dipped into night and they sat there in the half-dark, missing the stripes of light on the floor. Mark sat erect, straining to hear the gong, desperate to keep Tania's hopes high while she tipped her head back to yawn, then let her whole body sink back onto the pillows.

'I've been counting the trains,' Mark said. 'Shall we see how many minutes between them? I've brought my stop-watch.'

'How many seconds more like,' Tania said, picking at her lips. 'I'm sick of the room shaking. Anyway, we'll have to find this dining-room. My stomach's louder than the bloody express.'

Tania led the way, her cork soles squeaking. They'd almost missed the second sitting, they were told. They wouldn't be able to have the cauliflower soup, but they were just in time for the main course. That was the next best thing again, Mark thought with relief. We'll still have our dinner and Tania had already said she didn't like soup much when he'd shown her the menu for the evening. She would have liked the crusty roll and butter that went with it, though, because they only had sliced white at home.

'My Mum buys this braised beef,' Tania said. 'Frozen it is. Red packet. Really good.'

Her lips were glazed with gravy. Mark watched her add mashed potatoes and peas to the thin meat speared on her fork. He liked her good appetite. As she ate, her cheeks turned pink and soft. She needed her food.

He poured water and moved the salt closer to her, pleased that conversation didn't matter amid the clanking cutlery and the murmurs from other guests. It was expected in a guest-house that you ate without much speaking and watched your manners the time. Tania was inclined to rest her elbows on the table and swill her mouthfuls down with water, but Mark didn't mind. It was good to see her happy and anyway, they were sitting in a corner and her back was turned to the other guests.

While they waited for the semolina pudding, they listened to quiet talking about interest rates and in-laws and funerals. Every few minutes, a hot breeze billowed the net curtains like a bride's veil. Mark could have sat there forever.

They trooped into the lounge afterwards, following everyone else, but neither of them were used to drinking coffee. Mark didn't know whether to ask for tea, or if they were allowed to eat the thin chocolates fanned out on a dinner-plate.

They sat on a low sofa, Mark sweating in his badge-less blazer, his hands purple on his knees. No one talked to them. The men had cigars and beards and long-broken voices. Their world was set like a blancmange. It quivered at Mark's touch. But he couldn't penetrate it. He felt as if he were waiting at the end of a party, to be collected by an adult who had lost track of time.

He knew all the eyes swivelled in his and Tania's direction as they left the lounge, the same as going to the front of the class to read out an essay. Everyone looking and expecting and glad it's not their turn. The same burning up the spine because you know you haven't done a good job.

He wanted to go for a walk, but the straps of the borrowed sandals were biting into Tania's feet. And she said the streets were the same as home anyway.

She took off her clothes as soon as they were in the room. Mark turned to the window and studied the crisped woodlice lined up on the slats of the blind. He heard her drop her skirt and blouse onto the chair, heard the soft unrolling of her underwear. She slid under the sheet.

'I'll do my teeth after,' she said, yawning.

'Have you done this before?'

'Of course not.'

She crossed her arms, hugging the bedclothes over her body.

'I thought we'd do something first,' Mark said.

'Like what?'

'Maybe check the timetable for the train back. Or rinse out today's clothes.'

'Why do you reckon I've done this before?'

'The way you're being.'

'How am I being?'

'Like you know all about it.'

'You know this is the first time.' Her voice dropped to a whisper. 'Shouldn't have to tell you that.'

Mark watched her pick at her nail varnish.

'And the braised beef made you look more excited than being here in the room with me,' he said. 'It's like you're just going through the motions.'

'Well, it's a bit boring here, Mark. Nothing like the picture, is it? There's only one decent pillow. And these trains thundering past are getting on my nerves.'

They fell silent for a minute. The express rocked the walls.

Tania yawned, her mouth so wide that Mark thought it might be permanently hinged open. 'I thought there'd be wine,' she said at last.

'We can't, Tan. We're too young.'

She stared at him, her mouth sullen with scorn.

Mark glanced around as if he hoped a bottle of champagne would appear in a bucket of ice. He wondered if Tania were thinking the same and dragged out a laugh for her to share. But she didn't. Instead she let the sheet fall from her body, trapping it beneath her hands.

'Mark, are you going to do anything?'

He thought about his pyjamas, whether to put them on. Tania's flesh, drenched with her raspberry perfume, was waiting for him to touch it. Like the tender cuts of meat the butcher would handle tomorrow. She was patting the silky hummocks of the quilt, inviting him in.

Her bare skin was the same as clothes to her. She had sisters in her room at home. She was used to it. No one ever saw Mark in his. Tania's family shared themselves with each other. None of them kept secrets. The sisters would soon know all about Arlington Villas, if Tania thought there was anything to tell.

Mark looked at the slim rods of the bedstead. He didn't want to hear it thump against the wall. There were guests the other side. He and Tania might get into trouble for causing a disturbance of the peace. And in between the trains rushing by, the peace here was beautiful. Mark wished they could stay forever.

'It's been a long day, Tan. We should go to sleep. Early start tomorrow.'

'What the Hell was the point of this, Mark?'

'It's our special night away, Tan, isn't it? Just us.'

'Oh, great. Remind me to send a postcard before we catch the train.'

Tania lay down with a defeated sigh. Lorry brakes hissed by their window. Mark took off his blazer. He could smell his sour underarms, but he didn't know if they were allowed to run a bath. It might cost extra for hot water. He'd used every penny of his paper-round money and post-office savings to book this room and buy the train tickets. He would look like a fool if he couldn't pay the bill in the morning.

Tania's eyes closed. Her breathing deepened. He wished he could wipe off her mascara. It was staining the pillow with black peppery fragments. If she felt his tissue, she might take hold of his hand and pull him close. He wished he could lay his head on her breast and feel the soft underside of her arm cradle him to sleep.

He knew she'd be cross next day at school. She'd huddle by the lockers with Janice, who would shriek with disappointment.

He took out his needle, already primed with thread. He sewed the badge back onto his breast pocket, looking up now and again at the rise and fall of Tania's right shoulder. He would cover it with the sheet when he'd finished. It was chilly now. He'd be all right drowsing in the chair with his blazer draped over him, counting the trains as they flashed through the night.

He wouldn't need to count the stations they passed through tomorrow. Theirs was the final stop. The train wouldn't be going anywhere else.

Laura Seymour

The Last Dragon

You said you wanted to be a dragon
for Halloween. I imagined two shoeboxes
painted green with white cartoon teeth
see-sawing over your face,
funny googly eyes: a friendly dragon.

Yet when your pupils flashed coronets
of flame over your candy loot, I realised how,
in your mental mirror, you saw yourself:
as the last dragon, narcissistic asbestos curls
from its nostrils heating its lair
in the yapping basalts of Snowdonia,
blasting with blastoma any one nearby.

Your navel, caked over with pulsing scales,
erased from time:
you had never been tied to another.

The Capgras Delusion

The Capgras Delusion is a neurological condition which causes people to think that their loved ones, pets, and even places or objects, are cleverly-disguised impostors

I know what this is: cots of night scented stock:
knotted sheets tugged out with blood on.

I want to be in my house, not this house,
the one just like it, the original. Here
the stove's been repainted the same red, then aged artificially.

My sisters: when I see them, no sweat,
no bacteria's bluish love-in-idleness braids my skin
like selenite. I daub identifying pen covertly on their cuffs,
watch their shop-bought skin pucker, adding layers.

Orford Ness

When they netted black rubber frogmen
pulling torpedoes, for days later the birds survived
on seared femurs from the beach.

Spindly humanoids evade
in sodium coloured light: beach-combers have found
a luminous fingertip, a bubblewrap heart.

The man, a tangle of obsidian comb gaps
veins burning with the horse-kick of electricity
is coming back for more with the tide.

Music for the ministry

For this motorway, the Transport Ministry made us move
graves. Where squids like batteries once angled
beeping backbones, spirits tan, knock femurs jumble.

I bag up one collapsed in the hallway
fetching marmalade, tuppence a scoop
fifty pence left, no close living relatives.

One Emily buried a single, now evaporated, opera
glove right here, packed staining earth over rucked
moleskin. She'd never live as she did that evening.

Over my feet, two men dry stone walled for the verger
in 1853, testing oak like biceps against each
other, Cotswold stone white as brain pan rivers.

Here is the motorway, where before
a whale with gravity keened to no one hearing,
that you are now there is fossil rain unravelling.

Gabriel Griffin

The house-painters of Catal Huyuk

They moulded bulls' heads
on walls, leopards
in relief, stuck on
bones, horns, fangs.

As paints, oxides of iron:
browns, yellows, rust.

Bright blue was
azurite; grey, galena.

For red: cinnabar and haematite,
for green they pounded malachite. Black
was the soot from the fires.

But ochre they saved
for the sleeping dead
so they might dream their colourful dreams
buried in wicker baskets
under their own beds.

Ice Age Man

We have their cold
deep in our bone marrow, their hunger
in the pit of our stomachs, their gods
in the caves of our minds.

We'll never meet. I'll never
take your hand in mine, invite you
to my home; you'll never dine with me,
talk late into the night, share wine. You are
distant from me twenty thousand years or
more and what I see is just a grainy film
in faded blacks and whites and you—
a Bergman figure struggling through
deep snow, clambering into furrows, over
great ridges in the ice. You're but a smudge
on the white unwritten paper of the past.

Your cold, your hunger, isn't mine, nor
your days hunting in the snow, wolf
wary, alert for tiger, bison, bear, your
weapon only stone. Dusk you return
to where a fire has burned all day and they
wait for a gift of death, ensuring
their brief hope of life.

Should we meet, there would be
nothing we could say, your tongue, your
way of life, your landscape
alien to all I know. But I dream you sign
for me to follow and we go into your cave
past women, children eating, sleeping, loving,
telling tales, then deep inside the cracks and fissures
of the rock to where you've blown
pictures on the cavern's overhang and
dark, uneven walls. You've used ochre,
hematite, manganese ground fine
and soot from the saving fire
to recreate bison, horse, reindeer, auroch:
beasts that spring to life in your flame. I
put out my hand and fit it into yours, a print
left for me millennia ago on
the cavern's furthest wall.

A Little Gesture of Defiance

Marg Roberts

My mind uncurls from dreams into unfamiliar light. For several moments I lie buried in sleep, feeling the stillness. I stretch my legs between the cotton sheets, extend my feet into coolness. Winter breathes through the windowpanes, urging me to stir. I release the damp hanky from my clenched palm. I roll to the edge of the bed, push back top sheet and duvet, sit up before padding across the carpet to the window.

Snow is falling. The birdbaths, the path, even the wood panels of the gate are as thick as icing waiting to be sliced. The road has merged with the hedge. A girl again, I fling open the window. Cold drifts in, snowflakes melt on my fingers. I poke my head into the early morning, searching with my tongue. When I taste it, it tickles.

No one will travel up the lane this morning, which is a pity, because I feel like sharing this wonder. Snow is an excuse for wellies, winter coat, knitted hat and a two-mile walk into the village. I can chat to Minnie in the post office and on my way home call for a coffee at my friend Carole's.

I glance at the illuminated numbers on the clock radio. Eight o'clock. I resist the temptation to switch on the light and continue to watch.

It's Friday and the particular Friday I promised to help my son, Gerald, at the shop. I, who yesterday visited Dr. Fergusson about my memory lapses—why didn't I remember when I woke up?

I stir; shut the window and dash to the wardrobe. There are five pairs of trousers to choose from. Black with turn-ups I wear to school reunions. Jeans, tight round the waist. Velvet trousers I wore for evening functions before my retirement ten years ago and two pairs of slacks from Debenham's sale. There's a button missing on the green pair, so I pick the grey dogtooth.

I lay my underclothes and tights on the duvet. I could have warned Gerald marriage to Vanessa wouldn't work and to buy a business together was plain foolish. I went out of my way to be friendly, but she wasn't interested. In their first year, I took them twice to Oscar's, the only stylish restaurant in town, but Vanessa was sniffy about the veal and corrected the French spelling on the menu.

I pick up the photo of my daughter Violet on the dressing table and kiss it. My lovely girl.

I ought to move because the snow will delay me, but why? Enjoy the moment.

I yank at the dressing table drawer and grab the top jumper. It's a lime green polo neck I bought for fifty pence, two or three years ago at Oxfam. I place it on the trousers and hurry into the bathroom.

Ten minutes later, I'm downstairs in the living room. I check my purse is in my handbag, which I tuck behind a cushion on the settee each night, in case I'm burgled. Two pound fifty for Cross Street car park, a ten-pound note. That's more than enough for coffee and croissant from Starbucks.

I close the door and step into the porch, which smells of the lavender *pot pourri* Carole made. I reach for the boots on the rack next to the umbrella stand. They aren't there. This morning I hate Gerald. Another divorce; more money wasted. Dr. Fergusson had patted my hand and reassured me everyone forgets from time to time; she says there's a test a psychiatrist can do when I'm ready.

Ever since I moved out here when Ron died, I've worn slippers inside the house. The carpet is a light peach colour. Not practical, I admit, but I like it. I usually remove my outdoor shoes in the porch and put them on the rack. I'm wearing cream slippers; there are two pairs for visitors (large for men, small for women), so where are my shoes? It's part of being human, Dr. Fergusson said. To forget things.

I glance at my watch. Half past eight. How will I get the car out of the garage? I'll have to dig away the snow so that I can open the doors and the spade is in the potting shed at the bottom of the back garden. I'll be late. Gerald will be cross. I pull the keys from my bag, unlock the door and step back into the house. By now I should be leaving the car park and walking through The Priors on my way to Gerald's shop in Portland Street.

I hear his: - 'Mother! You do realise this is rush hour? '

I scurry back into the living room and poke my head in the cupboard under the stairs with no confidence of my shoes being there. I switch on the light expecting to see a vase I bought for Carole's birthday in April. It's only January, but it was in House of Fraser sale and I like to buy in advance when I can. There it is. Good. I'll report that to Dr. Fergusson. The torch in case there's a power cut, a pack of candles and a box of matches.

In the kitchen nothing is out of place. The draining board is spotless. The glass doors to the cabinets, which I clean each Tuesday morning, glisten; the cover to the cooker is down; the unused dishwasher bought by Gerald, still wearing its plastic sleeve. I contemplate looking upstairs, but I'd no reason to take my shoes there. My gardening shoes are by the back door, drying on a sheet of the Courier. They're covered in mud from Sunday when I dug up a clump of snowdrops to put in a pot on the windowsill, next to the photo of Violet being held by Ron at her christening.

I'll have to wear my gardening shoes. Mud or no mud. Thank God there'll only be Gerald to criticise. My head is racing and he'll want to rush: no doubt hoping Vanessa will forgive him.

At last I close the porch door. Cold invades me, seeps deep inside. My feet sink into snow on the step, which reaches an inch or two up my shins, chilling them. The low box hedge, which skirts the path, has gone. I wish I'd brought my camera. It would fix the scene forever. The old oak's branches are covered with snow; its dark trunk majestic in the blanketed countryside, while in the garden, the tiny laburnum is decorated with white loops.

Each time my shoe prints, I look back, admiring the way it holds its shape. Mud from my shoes soils the snow. Step by careful step, I reach the gate. I have a silly urge to build a snowman. I don't want to go to Gerald's shop, which is cold and draughty, where there won't be customers because he does most of his business on the Internet.

Snow has drifted four inches up the gate and no matter how hard I tug, it won't move. I dig a channel with the tip of my shoe, but even that doesn't shift it, so I trudge back into the house for the spade, a sick feeling crawling through my stomach, rising into my throat.

I'm about to do something I've never done before.

Back in the living room, I patter in my stocking feet across the carpet to the kitchen. Through the bay window snow spins out of control. How will I find the courage after years of pussyfooting? I'm drawn into the dizziness of the falling flakes and I steady myself against the edge of the sink. Violet, impassive in her father's arms, takes no notice.

After barely five minutes out of doors, I'm frozen. My fingers are numb as I turn on the hot water tap, listening as it gurgles down the plughole. I wince as feeling returns. I long to soak my feet and sit in front of the coal fire. Or build a snowman. Anything. I pick up the towel from the radiator, rub my hair. Furiously.

I move a dining room chair to sit on while I make the phone call, though I don't anticipate being long. The cuckoo bursts out of her thatched cottage, so there's no pretending it's not nine o'clock. Even if Gerald drove out for me, he'd be late for court. I'm tired.

Gerald is a long time answering and I'm tempted to ring off, but if I walk to the village and he discovers I'm not here, what then? Afterwards I can build the snowman. I've a straw boater in the wardrobe, coal, of course, for his buttons, brolly in the hat stand left behind by a long forgotten visitor.

'Mother!' Gerald bellows.

My hand is shaking so much I'm afraid I'm having an attack of some kind. Dr. Fergusson said I must make the most of my life.

I squeak, 'It's snowing.' He won't expect me to refuse so I must be firm. 'It's snowing and I can't get the car out.'

'I'll come over, if you like.'

Shall I tell him I don't want to help, that Dr. Fergusson agrees I may be losing my memory, that she'll send me for tests, but not to act precipitously?

'I don't want to come to the shop this morning, Gerald.'

There. I said it. Through the living room window the snow falls relentlessly. If I switched on the radio it would tell me how long it's been since we've had such a heavy fall.

'I know, Mother. It's bloody awful weather, but…' I don't listen.

I dread the idea of not remembering. Especially Violet. Ron used to say I worried too much.

'I know it's hard for you, but please...'

'I'm having a bad day.'

'I'll fetch you. You'll feel better with company.'

My knees begin to shake. 'No.' I hate the way he drives. He doesn't look at the road, but either chats to me or into the mobile.

'I'll catch the bus.'

I put down the phone. My little gesture of defiance.

The gate released by a few strikes of the spade, my confidence returns. As a child I walked everywhere with my parents and snow was a treat. It squeaks under my shoes as I stride along the lane towards the main road. My eyes water with the constant swirl of snow. I was a teacher at the school when Violet ran across the road after eight-year-old Gerald and was killed by a car. Mr. Wilson, the headmaster, allowed one week's compassionate leave; he admired resolute women. But when Ron left me, in the summer of the same year, he never mentioned it.

My bones are frozen and I walk stiff as crutches. I remember Gerald rang me. My memory's not as bad as I feared.

I lose track of time. It usually takes ten minutes to reach the main road. Perhaps twenty in these conditions. There's still no traffic, only a few bird and animal footprints. I can walk to Carole's. She'll give me a lift to the village in their 4 x 4.

At last, at last, I've reached the start of the gravel drive to Carole's. From here, I work out where it ought to meet the main road and I plunge straight into its drifts. My jaw has merged into my neck and shoulders; I can only look ahead. I came to hate Mr. Wilson. He didn't like my telling the children about the snowman who disappeared when his mummy gave him a hot water bottle. I round the bend and see smoke, like serpents rising, from the tall chimneys.

I wore this jumper yesterday while I made Christmas puddings, packing them in tin foil, sticking on sellotape labels to identify which friends they were for. I drag my legs up the drive to the house. Men don't like women wearing trousers in my experience. The snow swims in front of my eyes and I yearn to be picked up and carried. I concentrate on putting one foot into the snow, steadying myself, then the other, forcing myself to stay upright, not giving in to the temptation to crawl.

Strength evaporates as soon as my fingers leave the bell. I collapse on the clean step and lean into the porch wall. I smell baking—cakes or biscuits—and I'm clutching Carole's arms as she hoists me to my feet. My jaw is rigid. I shuffle over the parquet floor, not stopping to remove my shoes, afraid I'll not move again if I do. My feet shrink, my mind with them. Carole grips my hand so tight I find it hard not to cry out.

'Where's your coat?'

No coat. I've forgotten my coat. I must not forget Violet. Five-year-old Violet. Every nerve pulsates with pain as we skirt the oak table. A cut glass vase overflows with snowdrops from the woods behind the house. I'm pushed onto a wooden chair. The muscles in my bottom ache and I drop my shoulders onto the table, allow my head to rest on my arms. I try to apologise for the melting snow and the way it's marking the red tiles, but no words form.

'Where's your coat?' Carole is angry.

I flap an arm and another layer of snow slips from my shoulder to the floor. I try to catch it, but it eludes me.

'He doesn't believe me,' I say.

'Who?'

I can't remember. Carole kneels at my feet and unfastens one of the shoelaces.

'What in the world were you thinking?'

I close my eyes. *I don't believe you.* Mr. Wilson's voice comes back. I hadn't gone to school because we were snowed up so I missed the school inspector's visit. The inspector, a Mr. Bowland I recall, spotted Mr. Wilson relied on me. That's what turned him against me.

Carole says, 'I'll have to cut them.'

She stands up, wipes her hands down her apron and I notice rows of buns on cooling trays by my elbow.

'Gerald.' Thank God, I can speak. It must be dreadful to be imprisoned in a mind, which has things to say, but no words with which to say them. 'Gerald needs me.'

'Gerald needs you?'

Carole marches across the tiles, her slippers flapping. She comes back with scissors and snips the laces on both shoes in seconds. She's never liked Gerald. My shoe crashes to the floor.

'Mary.' This time her voice is kind.

My foot is white. It doesn't belong to me.

Carole crouches, lifts my left foot and rests it on her knee. She rubs it with both hands as though trying to set it alight. The pain stops me composing a sentence that will please her. I grip the edge of the chair, hold my breath, smell the warm sweetness of the buns.

'Could you give me a lift?'

'Bill will take you back when he gets home. In the meantime, you soak in a hot bath, have a lie down and then a bit to eat. I've made some soup. Plenty for us both.'

The blood stirs in my foot and I wriggle my toes. I watch the pool of water flicker on the red tiles.

'She was a good girl,' I say.

'She was.'

'Have I told you I was a teacher and Mr. Wilson was the head?'

'It was an accident.'

'She loved her brother.'

Carole straightens, her hand in the small of her back. Her expression is grim. I press my bare foot on the floor, shift it an inch or so and see the blur beneath it.

Carole tucks her hair behind her ears, thrusts her face so close I smell the garlic on her breath. She clasps my hands, lowers her head and covers the backs of my hands with kisses. I shiver.

'Now the other foot,' she says.

'You don't have the car?'

'I'll give that son of yours a piece of my mind.'

Carole doesn't understand.

'You can't take me then?'

I gaze at the grey hairs on the top of her head as she removes my other shoe, rubs the foot. I am getting used to the hurt. At all costs Gerald mustn't know I'm not the ticket.

'What time is it?'

'You're not going.'

'I could order a taxi.'

'You're not going.'

Carole has three healthy sons, two have been to university, the youngest is doing well. She has a devoted husband and her parents live in Australia.

She pats my knee and stands up. 'I'll run the bath.'

When she's gone I bend down and stroke my feet. I used to paint the nails, rub cream into them every night. The shoes are wet, the laces trail on the floor like worm casts, but I force myself to push my feet in. I hate the idea of going out into the cold. I listen to Carole's footsteps on the wooden stairs, the creaking overhead. She'll be making up the spare bed. I long to sit with her as I have many times and reminisce about Violet.

I wade in wet shoes. My feet are numb. I drag myself away from the smell of buns. I tell myself it's something I have to do in order to survive, to keep Violet alive.

At the front door, my fingers stumble with the Yale lock. I turn it a fraction at a time, listening out for Carole. Water is running into the bath. I clench the damp hanky in the palm of my hand. I open the door on the falling snow.

Andie Lewenstein

Communion

In my mother's husband's house empty wine bottles stand greenly in the hall like passengers
in transit from one train to the next, unsure if they are on the right platform. We edge
between them when going from one room to another but I must not move them because he does not want me to decide where things should be when I am in his house. He waits for me to speak. Each word is scrutinised. *It is a nice day. You say so, do you?*

We have Gunpowder tea from Fortnum and Mason, leaves kept in the pot for several brewings. After the fifth, one tastes only the chlorine of tap water, though there is still a trace of yellow which resembles pale urine. He wants to know if I appreciate the tea. I suspect this is a joke but am never sure. My mother hovers, fetches tins of stale biscuits and then removes them. He says sit down but prefers her not to. No-one should be at ease. He is at ease and takes a slice of cake from the special tin which has been shipped from Germany. I reminisce about my grandmother's Sachertorte, a fusion of marmalade and *zartbitter schokolade*. My mother's husband says I am wrong about the marmalade. I recite a list of German cakes: *Sandkuchen, Windbeutel, Mohnkuchen, Linzertorte, Marmorkuchen, Streuselkuchen, Bienenstich.*
My mother's husband hates the litany.

He tells my mother to open a bottle of red wine. His spirits, invariably low, are lifted. I see how it consoles him. He offers me a glass and speaks about its lineage, the subtle notes that I might miss because I am not a connoisseur. Wine is something he loves with a pure heart.

He lifts his glass to catch the gleam. *The blood of Christ*. No-one says this. There is just my pity coupled with his relenting for the length of time it takes to finish a bottle—some apprehension that, in the teeth of evidence stacked against us, we might love each other.

Martin Willitts, Jr.

Calligraphy Brush

It is said, first woman sang cherry blossoms
until a horse emerged out of the mists. It is said,
she took hairs from its tail, which went here
to there, further than a dragon's fire, further
than blossoms float in strong wind as tiny fans.
It is said she used the hairs to make the first brush,
like whispers of her eyelashes, softer than mist.
She drew a horse chasing freedom, its tail on fire,
spreading the scent of blossoms there to here.
It is said that first word was made this way.
Each word falling scales from a shedding dragon.
It is said, this is how stars were made from ink.
Who says these things? Lies float petals,
here and there, swishing truth at mayflies

Dip your brush into plum blossom ink,
make the mark for the word of woman
onto rice paper from the forbidden garden.
Your words mist, gallop out of paper,
flapping dragon wings delicate as a woman's lashes.

Lies float there to here, near paper lanterns, as moths.

How to Recover from Loss into Light

"For me, everything was too much, and nothing was enough" —Mary Karr, Facing Altars: Poetry and Prayer

What exactly is gracious or especially tragic
and unsung about a hurtling death?
You had enough of nothing
having wrung the essence out—
like a cold getting out of bed, dehydrated—
life is too much of everything
but not enough of anything;
never enough, never, never prayer—

ignoring small blessings; the scarce air;
the restless resonating tiny inner voices
like rippling pebbles from the cauldron
of abundance. Never enough for you, but sufficient
to see the edge between enough and not enough—
a wedge between uncertainty and belief.

Instead—try filling, tossing earth unto earth,
filling that cavity in the heart. Try
dark earth, the kind earthworms prefer.
Try moss-smelling soil, enriched nitrate
filings of dirt, rich as lavender soap. If that fails,
if you still feel like failure—try mud,
try straw, dry crumbling leaves, compost,
rejection letters that liter the heart. Fill—
until it mounds, like fairy mounds
in Africa created by termites. Build monoliths
like Stonehenge slabs, teeth gnawing at light.
Construct ziggurats, towers for Nimrod, escape
limits of language into a frenzy of silence.
Find awe is just too unnamable.

When your arms become the spade
mouthing absolute light and dirt,
toss more muck onto the pain.

Prue Chamberlayne

Raptor

I stumble up a steep and scraggy slope on animal tracks
towards a burst of blossom choked by undergrowth

thoughts on my parents' wedding, the church in Tirley banked
with this same prettiness, decay and war impending,
and how to reach the apple tree for cutting,

when just behind a bush I'm standing by—I only see a smudge—
there's smacking, shuddering, a lift of massive weight by rush of wings.

I'm quivering with loss, mind captured by departed presence
a being who lives well here, reads signs I miss, he must have
watched with nervous glances, picked the ground with furry ankles,

not staying to be possessed by my regard. I carry on
encased in brambles and what I hadn't known was closely there.

Houndstor

From high banked lanes we cross a grid
to gorse, bronze bracken and shorn grass,
and they come rearing over the brow.

Not till we're right among them
does their living presence breathe,
impel on us their making—

eased up from cauldrons,
tossed here by gods, sledged in by glaciers,
stacked by giants as megalithic slabs.

We peer at cracks and splits, protrusions
outlasting wind and rain—Kapoor's piled turds,
hunched couple, an Easter Island boxer's nose.

You, so young, with skinny legs
reach over crevices, defy the tilting
to stand astride these moors,

wave to a falcon hovering,
while I, as clouds press drizzle,
steal glances at a far off golden slope.

Salad Days
Zoe Swenson-Wright

My first job of the morning is to bleach the salad. It's all yellowed and soft at the edges from yesterday's lunch and night in the refrigerated larder, so I fill, as I always do, the large salad sink with water and tip in the bleach. Then in goes the brownish lettuce to swill around for ten minutes or so until sepia turns to green and the limp edges have plumped up. They are still soft and a bit soggy-tasting but they look fine. Never eat a wet-looking cafeteria salad. Actually mine is not wet-looking because I'm a perfectionist and have introduced the practice of spinning it dry. The spinner is not very big so it takes about five loads to finish the whole salad, but the end result is excellent. I showed it to the catering manager and he said I was demonstrating real initiative and had a solid future ahead of me.

I wouldn't eat second day salad myself, but it won't hurt you. We are very safety-conscious in this kitchen and throw it away after the second day, even if there's a ton left. The bleach would work a few more times, I think, but our standards are pretty high.

I have to get up at 5:30 every morning for this job, so that breakfast can be ready by 7:00. I just do breakfast and lunch, preparing cold dishes and serving them. I'm done by 3:30 in the afternoon and at first I thought I'd have lots of free time but I'm always exhausted and sleep for hours afterwards. I have a room here at the hotel. In fact, that is why I am still in this job. I have run away from everything: home, college, success, my future. If there's anything left at the end of that list, I guess I'll find it eventually.

Right before I decided to leave home it just hit me: I don't know why my parents are paying for all this, but it has to stop. I acted like everything was fine and packed my usual suitcase for college, except that inside was everything I thought I'd need to cope on my own. And that feeling—the scared, excited feeling when I bought my bus ticket to nowhere—maybe that was worth losing a future for, because it was amazing.

On my second to last day at home, I used my credit card to take out a huge amount of money so that I could get by for a couple of months without being traced. After five hours driving on the Interstate, the bus stopped at a rest station next to a flattened-out, one-story motel called the Sundown Motor Plaza. It was painted bright yellow, like a kid's paint box, with blue windows and curtains. Despite being sort of run down, the motel looked like something out of a cartoon. The sort of place that salesmen and truckers like, where every room has its own front door and parking slot.

Why we stopped was to use the rest area, which had bathrooms, a gas station, a candy and magazine store and a cafeteria. I took my suitcase to the ladies' room because I wanted to change clothes and when I came out, the bus was gone and I was there on my own.

At first I was really angry but then I thought, well what difference does it make if I wasn't going anywhere special? So I walked into the Sundown Motor Plaza and booked myself a room and they seemed so excited, as if I was the first person to book a room in weeks. The one they gave me was right at the end of the parking lot and so quiet and private, all my own. I had a really long shower and watched TV for a bit. Then I walked around to the back of the hotel, where there was a little playground for kids, with swings and a slide, and nothing much beyond, just fields and a derelict warehouse. You couldn't even see the Interstate.

I made my way over to the cafeteria and had a burger and fries and they were pretty good. This was just the kind of rest area my parents would *never* come to, even if my brother was throwing up or desperate for the bathroom. 'Just pull over on the side of the road,' my Mom would say. 'Go behind those trees.'

So I went to talk to the cafeteria manager, whose name is Dave. He was excited too—they'd had a catering assistant job advertised for weeks and no one had applied—'we're way off the beaten track,' he said. I took the job right away and Dave helped me negotiate with the hotel so I could pay a long-term cheap rate for my room, like someone renting an apartment. And here I still am, fugitive from life.

Once I started hiding, it became an obsession. Dave gave me a ride into town, seven miles away, and I used my new work name to open a bank account. I thought they'd ask more questions but the girl behind the counter was really shy and I had this huge envelope of cash and kept saying I was in a hurry, so she just did it. After that, I cut up the old credit card and lived on what I earned. I've bought a disposable phone but I don't have anyone to call. The long term plan is to move up in the job, maybe run my own hotel some day. The people are great here, especially Dave, who's really young to be the catering manager; most who work for him in the kitchens are older. He thinks I could be a success.

What's great is being invisible. Except for the truck drivers, the people who use this cafeteria barely look at you. It's like they are ashamed to be here. They mumble their orders and peer around at other people to make sure there's no one they know. They pig out on the first half of whatever they ordered, then get embarrassed and wrinkle up their noses at the rest. As if it was so gross they couldn't face it, although actually our portions are pretty large and most people can't finish.

Invisibility suits me, except that sometimes it's hard to feel good about your day when other people are looking down their noses. It bothers me most when they do it to Dave because he's so proud of this place and keeps the standards really high. When I see that happen, it helps to think: *someday I'll be manager at a fancy hotel and you'll ask for a favor and I'll say no, not you. Because before I was so successful I served salad at the Sundown Motor Plaza and you acted like we all had bugs or something.*

Last week, I was on my break in the staff room, where the TV's really loud, and everyone was laughing about this guy who bought a bleached, blow-dried weasel thinking it was a kitten. The weasel acted weird around his house, so after a few days he took it to the vet. All very funny but they didn't say what happened to the weasel, with its eager little face in the TV photo. You just know the vet put it to sleep, don't you? Just for being itself. And probably right when it was settling in and thinking, what a great home, it's such a blast living here.

Sometimes life is just a random, pointless drag. But it's better than before, when my world was starting to feel really, really out of control. Living at the Sundown and working at the cafeteria, I can keep things pretty smoothed out and that helps with the day-to-day.

A few nights ago, I dreamt I'd had the baby and the nurse put it into my arms all wrapped up in a blue blanket, and it was a lovely little pale thing with its hair slicked back and its eyes closed. And as I rocked it, it began to dry off and the hair puffed up not only on top of its head but on its cheeks and neck and ears and then it opened its eyes and they were bright little beads darting about. It started to wriggle and scratch in my arms as if it was trying to get away and I woke up panting and sweating.

If you don't know what happened it's because of my parents who pressured and bribed everyone involved to keep it out of the college newsletter and away from campus security and the police. To be fair, my Dad wanted to go to the police at first but I couldn't get my story together. I was honestly so drunk that night I couldn't remember anything that happened and both guys said the same. We actually woke up all together, pretty much undressed and bruised and vomiting in a room I'd never seen before. The Social Dean for my class wanted to follow the 'official procedure for serious incidents' but all three sets of parents went to her in a group and said no, it wasn't good behaviour but it wasn't rape. So we three were sent home for the spring semester to recover from 'stress' and had to promise that we hadn't videoed anything and wouldn't talk about it. There was some gossip, but less than you'd think because we hardly knew each other before and didn't have overlapping friends. Salvageable, from my parents' point of view. I'm making them sound pretty cold, but they were trying, really. Of course they got all my course plans and found an academic tutor so that I could keep up. They renewed my gym membership too—I spent hours in the pool, hot tub and steam room. And it was plain sailing for a couple of months until I started throwing up right after breakfast.

I thought they'd completely freak but they were actually OK about it. We talked about the medical procedure and I read some chapters in a book, and then we went to a Clinic attached to a women's center and it was all just as described. I felt really sick before and almost as bad after, but I stopped throwing up in the morning. Just one more unexpected hurdle to jump en route to my successful life.

Timewise, it worked out fine. I was fixed up in plenty of time to get ready for the Fall semester. I'd been texting my friends all summer, planning what we were going to do. And then these other pictures started taking over. A little house where I made things ready. A baby opening its eyes. How all the correct decisions had been made and my life was a fine, rational place to go back to, but I couldn't, because I wasn't actually me any more.

I didn't say it to anyone. I wasn't attention-seeking, far from it. It was just a fact. Even in the mirror. I recognized my face, of course, but just couldn't match it to anything from before, like Facebook photos. I guess features aren't just bone and skin but the way you use your muscles to talk or smile. My old face was a glossy sort of smooth thing, very rounded. My new face was narrower, with a different set to the mouth especially, but I think something about the eyes too. One point that really clinched it for me was that my hair didn't fit anymore. I always used to have the perfect hair, everyone said that. Really thick and dark, with just the right amount of wave. The hair hadn't changed at all, but on this new face, it looked like a wig. Sometimes I'd walk past a store window and see it all tilted over to one side.

I never made a choice—I just started to understand where things were headed. Since there was no point freaking out my parents, I played along with all their plans and packed my bags and waved goodbye at the train station, still grinning and pretending. But at the first big interchange, I got off and took the bus.

And sitting on the bed in my new room at the Sundown, I felt really guilty and awful. I had to tell myself over and over that there was no other way. Because it never would have worked. I couldn't have fooled my school friends, for one thing. They would have taken one look at me and said, 'Who are you? A friend of ours is supposed to have this room.' And there would have been a scandal worse than before.

Dave always looks out for me. I know I'll be promoted before the end of the year. He asks questions and I don't mind when it's him because I know he likes the way I am. Dave's a local guy—really close to his family, who all live in the town, even his grandmother and cousins. Because of that, he sometimes asks, 'where's *your* family?'

'I don't really have one,' I say.

'You know,' he says, 'it's important to make it up with people, even if they've done something wrong. Everybody needs a home base.'

'I'll get by. It's just one of those things.'

'There must be someone you're mad at,' he says.

But there honestly isn't and I say so.

At first, the hair bothered me a lot. For the kitchen, of course you have to tie it up and wear a cap but the bits falling out at the sides looked dark and snaky and I worried that the whole thing would slide off into a salad and I'd be bald in front of everyone. So I found out where the cake girl and some of the cleaning ladies went to have their hair done and now I look pretty similar. It's blond and just above shoulder length. It is perfect with the new face and perfect with the cap and apron too. Dave didn't love it at first, but he's used to it now. It's incredible to have the right hair again. It can blow in the wind without blowing away.

When my parents finally went to the police, Dave called me in. 'This girl,' he said pointing to a newspaper missing person mugshot. 'She looks a bit like you.'

I snuck a glance at the photo and could have laughed with relief. It was of someone I barely recognized. I looked at Dave in sheer disbelief.

'No way. She doesn't look anything like me! Not even like a relative.'

He studied the photo again, 'Really? You don't think so? I mean, before you had your hair cut.'

'Completely totally different,' I said. 'I mean look at the shape of her face, and the way her mouth is.'

'OK, I guess I can see that.'

'And she's really thin. Look at her fingers.'

'But when you first came…'

'I guess her hair's kind of like mine used to be, but mine wasn't natural.'

'OK, OK. I just wanted to check.'

'You really think I look like that?'

'I just… No. of course not. You're *you*.'

'Yeah...' I didn't want to overreact but I was breathing really hard. I guess I was crying a little too.

'Hey,' he said. 'I didn't mean to upset you.'

'I'm OK.' I said. 'It's just…I mean…I thought you knew me.'

Dave put his arm around my shoulders, really heavy and warm. 'It's OK,' he said. 'Of course I do.'

'I'm just being stupid,' I said. 'I mean, thanks for worrying and everything. In case she was me.'

'No problem,' he said, looking relieved. 'I just thought there was a sort of resemblance, and you know, given how you showed up here.'

'That's nice of you, thanks.' I said. 'And no worries.'

I am spinning the salad extra carefully this morning, taking time over it, but Dave doesn't notice.

'What happened last night?' he asks. 'Where were you?'

'I'm really sorry—I had this terrible migraine.'

'I knocked on your door.'

'It happened when I was taking a walk. And I couldn't call because my phone went dead.'

It's a bullshit excuse and we both know it.

'My sister was looking forward to meeting you,' he says. 'Her kids made these special brownies.'

'I'm really, really sorry. I wanted to meet them too.'

And it was true. Up until the last minute it had been such a happy picture in my mind: me at his sister's, bouncing the baby, sipping at a glass of wine. All of us laughing at something the kids were doing.

'I just couldn't think with the migraine,' I say. 'I had to lay down in the grass and wait it out.'

He must see something real in my face, because he softens.

'I'm sorry about that,' he says. 'You missed a good night.'

'I bet.'

'Nice job on the salad.'

'Oh yeah, thanks!'

But he's turning away, checking out the cake girl, and her muffins going into the oven.

Kathleen M. Quinlan

Journeying through Fog

The paddles crack the silence
with rhythmic plunk and plash,

pull me sightlessly through whiteness.
I navigate by faith and the vague feel

of the current's suggestion. Suspended
rain, hanging between sky and river,

soaks my clothes, leaves droplets
on my cheeks. Blurred trees lurk

just beyond focus, their branches
camouflaged in a darker shade of grey.

The river's darjeeling scent mingles
with my coffee-tinged breath—now in,

now out—in unison with movement of
arms and shoulders striding into each

moment as murky as the last.
As my mind tires of striving,

I see a shape on the shore—
a dock or stopping place? I coast closer,

hoping. But black words emerge
on pale-painted board, warning,

No mooring.

Fourteen Dance Lessons

1. Admission

Write about dancing, you urge.
But when I try, I find
a mound of discarded CDs stands
between me and fifteen years
of Friday nights, wire brushes
on suede-soled shoes,
swirling skirts, and sweaty shirts.

2. Cha-Cha-Cha

It's not him stopping my pen—
My fear that I might conjure him,
his aggressive lead or pelvic thrust,
his pivot turns or twining grapevines.

It's not that he'll take another woman's
hand, pull her to his embrace, plant his hips on hers,
grind her to swooning here in my kitchen.

Or that he'll barrel-roll solo through
a roomful of stares, erupt into something
like song as I blush, hide, pretend he's not
the one who brought me, the one who will
claim the last waltz.

He's not spinning me to dizziness,
directing my feet, stealing my voice.

3. Foxtrot

It was an escape from words, from ideas,
from my workaday life of the mind.
A retreat to body, sweat, rhythm, grace,
where meeting, loving, parting—a whole romance,
a whole life—fit into three unrepeatable minutes.

And if I didn't like it, I could try again with another,
striving for that place where there is no striving,
when I'm so fully there I'm no longer there
in that darkened gymnasium with a DJ
and two hundred strangers, but

instead

gliding along a leaf's petiole,
sliding like a dew-drop
over an apple's curve,
caught in flight on milkweed silk.

4. A glass of water

How, then, do I crawl back
from that world without words

to a world made of words?
How do I find a rhythm

where there's no music,
feel a beat with no drum?

How can a mere scratch of pencil across page
move your feet, your hips, your heart?

5. Waltz

In my mind, it's all grace, fluid ease like birds in flight.

But the videos tell a different story, here a toe leading instead
of heel, there a slant to the arabesque,
the ronde's sweep smaller than remembered,
an awkward mis-step recorded for posterity,
mistakes frozen in time, never to be corrected.

6. Flamenco

When he was gone
I owned my limbs, no longer
antennae to his signals,
hands tamed in his grip.

Now arms—long and lean in a solo act—
can fling or flourish; hold skirts or veils
or castanets; swirl threads of mist,
paint invisible fences.

7. Sitting it out

I no longer dance.
Saying it hurts my feet
is no lie.

But I wonder if I'll forget, or if—
when the music starts and a new partner
takes my hand—it will be like picking up a thread,
following it through layers of grey folds
rising and falling, as natural
as breathing.

8. Quickstep

But we write together—share poems
with words that pivot and turn
like dancers, plot lines holding tension
like a ballroom frame,
here moving swiftly down the line,
there pausing for a graceful developpé,
a hesitation turn, building up to a running finish.

9. Paso Doble

Perhaps I didn't want to be the cape anymore,
red dress whipping and spinning under the matador's
hand, swirling across the floor, falling limp
as he raises his arms in triumph.

10.Tango

Maybe I tired of the coy game,
always keeping my head turned, eyes averted,
being that teasing temptress in some Argentinean bar,
parading through a mating ritual as arcane as
those creatures featured on National Geographic TV,
flicking and hooking, fanning and falling away—
ambivalent choreographies
of dominance, submission.

11.Ladies' Choice

With you, I listen to other music:
deeper, older, more complex.
It rolls over me like velvet balls,
falls silky across my shoulders,
grasps my diaphragm with kid
leather gloves, steers my mind
into feasts, conquests, funerals.

A different kind of universal.

12.Bolero

Understand that its *flow*, a term I learned
in some psychology book:

when you're on the edge,
pushing the limits of what you've
ever done and it's all clicking:
balance stable even through the slow,
sensual movements, not a falter on
the abrupt stops and starts;
two bodies feeling the same beat,
the same suggestion of the next move
so the music is leading, not him.

I slide my foot across the floor
away from the leading man,
pause that perfect instant as if I might
walk right out of the scene. Then, the heartbeat
when I swivel with a commanding snap:
the femme fatale, the big screen star returns,
hips first into his arms.

Everyone's watching now, caught up in the vortex—
the risk of muscle and pride and privacy;
the drama and heat. Nothing held back.

In my mind's eye my back flexes
like a gymnast as he lowers
me backward, straddling his bent knee,
                    sweeping me in a half circle
                                        to the point of lift.
My core pressing through hips ripples me up
to come nose to nose with the hero, each knowing in some
unspoken place exactly where to find the other
in physical space, breathing space, musical space.

The spin before the grand finale—
hitting the last note, nailing the last drop,
hearing the bystanders' spontaneous applause,
knowing
it doesn't get any better than this.

13.Salsa

Yes, of course, there was adrenaline:
a runner's high you might say,
killing the pain, fuelling the frenzy.

But it was still *real*. Real as rain
drumming on the windows.
Real as sleeping on a train,
the sound and feeling
of the rocking merging
so you don't know
which sense is which,
miles and towns blurring.

14.The Last Waltz

It's like when light bursts through a half-open door
and spring strides in, singing a familiar tune,
wearing her showy costume, trailing perfume.

No, it's like writing when the words fall on the page
like candy spilling from a piñata—except the flush
of treasure comes from some hidden source,
guiding you so your job is just
to listen, feel, channel.

This, my dear, is what it's like to dance.

Watershed

Come with me
and I'll take you to the two-faced
mountain with one foot in the snow,
another in the sun. Choose a leaf
and let it fall—like a tear—into the creek
that meanders Northward through the watchful
forest and ice-chiselled lakes to an unbridled
river that submits to the Eastern sea.

Come with me
and I'll show you another way.
Watch a leaf choose me and leap
from my hands like a dancer
into the ever-changing falls
tumbling somersaults Southward
in the spirited current
to a sweeping, salty bay.

Come with me
and we'll hold hands
over the Great Divide.
We'll imagine these two leaves
going forth—each in its own direction—
reunited in a wave
on some secret shore.

Hitler Was An Artist Too

David Frankel

The smoke black wall of the Methodist church is close enough to the fence for the water running from its broken gutter onto the cobbles of the store's back yard. Three of us lean on our brooms, smoking thin cigarettes, trying to keep warm and simultaneously remain inactive. *Minimum wage, minimum effort.* The motto of the unofficial union of Saturday boys. We stare over at the church's drizzle softened posters, and Wayne reads their slogans aloud: 'God is Love' and 'Jesus is Coming' to which somebody had added '...so look busy'. He starts building up for a sarcastic comment but tenses and hisses, 'Jesus. He's coming.'

Alan and I stare at him.

'Burt. Burt's coming.' He nods urgently toward the back door of the store.

My neck hairs bristle, three half smoked rollies fly over the wall in perfect formation and brooms hiss against the cobbles.

'Morning, Burt.'

'Haven't you lot finished yet? Move yourselves; I've got other things for you to do inside. And I want one of you to clean my car later.' He's looking at me. He doesn't know yet, I can tell. I haven't told anyone except the office staff and they don't speak to the rest of us if they can help it. I have worked here for exactly one year. This is my last day.

Burt scuttles back indoors, his bow-legged stride making his torso swing from side to side. 'Get a move on.'

As soon as he's gone tobacco and rizlas come out again.

'How come he likes you so much?'

I show Alan two fingers and say, 'He hates us all equally,' but I know what he said is true; Burt does like me. He considers it a treat to be allowed to wash his car instead of working in the warehouse. In summer, it is. Today it's freezing so he will probably make Wayne do it. He's liked me from the start. Since he found me sketching on my tea break. *Think you're Picasso do you?* Sticking his beak over my shoulder. *It's rubbish that.* But later on, out of sight of the others, he winked at me. *Good to have a bright lad like you on the team.* Even when he caught me skiving off, kipping in one of the sheds, he'd turned a blind eye. The tight old git docked my wages but he'd sacked people for less.

It pisses Wayne off something bad; 'I don't know how you get away with it. I've been here miles longer than you. You bastard.'

As far as I can tell it makes fuck all difference whether Burt likes me or not; he treats me the same as he treats everyone else; like something he's scraped off his shoe. Burt doesn't even own the place; he just runs it as though he does. He swans around like he's God or Jesus or the Dalai fucking Lama. The real owners are the Mason brothers. Well known locally. Quiet men, happy to hide behind Burt and keep their heads down while he does their dirty work. Neither knows the names of their employees. We are just blurred numbers printed on the thin paper of the wage slips they begrudgingly sign off each week.

The building was a department store once. Easily the grandest shop in town. Over two grabbing generations the Masons acquired the shops either side and knocked through. The building extended, expanded, filled, and was added to again, never quite re-designed, sagging under the weight of its own bulk. Their offices are hidden from the punters at the top of a narrow staircase. From there, the brothers preside over the selling of wallpaper, paint and tiles, bought and sold on the cheap, catering for the budget end of the market; patrons unburdened by money or taste.

Later, back inside, Burt is with me in the tea room, where the taste of fag ash, like spent gunpowder, clings to every cup and plate. He's smoking his cheap cigs. Really going for it, sucking hard on the fag and blasting the smoke back out, sitting in a cloud of fumes like Old Nick. He's ignoring me and I him. This is the setting for most of his crimes. I've seen him hovering before, with his bony little paws set like traps, waiting for one of the shop girls to stumble in. Maybe they're afraid they'll get the boot, but something makes them put up with his creeping mits. *You're looking very nice today. Pretty as a Renoir. Give your Uncle Burt a cuddle. How about a little kiss?* As soon as they reach for a cup, he's on them; quick as murder, dirty as sin. All made too easy by short skirts or torn jeans worn to impress the boys in the warehouse.

Today I see the trap's been set, so I stay. He's hardly the shy type but he's unwilling to perform in front of an audience. When Claire comes in I'm glad I stayed. She doesn't fit here. Too classy. From the new houses at the far end of town. But there's something else about her that seems out of step with her surroundings. The boredom and the grubbiness around us sharpens the effect she has on me.

She gets a sly hand on her arse as she passes him. I take my time and light a second cigarette to show I'm not moving and finally he retreats, angry but unable to complain, face like a fist; hard, screwed shut.

'Hurry up with that fag young man. I've got things for you to do.'

I'll have to pay for it later, but she smiles at me as I put my cold tea on the draining board. When I leave she takes the cigarette from my hand and finishes it.

Burt stands watching me while I wash his car in the rain. I can hear the rain drops on his umbrella and from the corner of my eye I can see his shoes on the cobbles as I bend to dip the sponge in the bucket. The rain running down the collar of my jacket is cold. The water in the bucket is colder. I pretend I haven't noticed him watching me. We've been through this routine a dozen times. He pretends he isn't punishing me and I pretend I don't care. I know what's on his mind but he doesn't say anything for a long time.

'They don't mind you know, the girls here.' With a wink in his voice that says we are both men of the world, he tells me, 'They love it. It's all they think about. They don't look at things the way we do. None of that lot in there do.' He nods toward the shop, 'Not artists. Not thinkers. No sensitivity.'

I don't say anything but I know he's right, partly at least. They don't like 'thinkers' around here. In this town ideas get boiled in lead until they're too heavy to draw breath. I remember the first time he told me about his secret life as a painter. Back when I was still green, I thought that made him okay. Meant he saw things differently. Meant he was better than the others. I know that's all bollocks, now. But I have to get away from this place, this town. It feels like it's stalking me. Waiting for me to relax, pause for long enough for it to lure me in and make me forget that I was ever going to leave.

When he's gone away, relieved by the opportunity to explain himself, I smoke a fag and head back indoors.

Above the faded glory of the main show rooms are two floors, each with over a dozen rooms full of shelves that are slowly collapsing, spilling boxes into ziggurats of discontinued stock. The contents of these rooms are incomprehensible to anyone but Lindsey and Stella. They spend six days a week locked together in mutual loathing, competing for control of the stock. Lindsey alternately beams at customers and glowers down the aisle at Stella whose face twists between silent rage and a nervous need to please. Only they know the locations of the goods that belong to the mysterious product codes.

I wait while they argue about what stock they want me to bring down to the shop floor, avoiding any eye contact or facial expressions that might be interpreted as taking a side. A list of instructions is scrawled in pencil onto a sample of patterned wallpaper and snatched back and forth as they argue about its contents. Their voices merge into one stream: *That one's in the back store—no it isn't its upstairs—well it shouldn't be. Who put it there?—I did. If I take the delivery I say where it goes—and what if I need to find it —you can ask…*

While they bicker, Claire stands behind them running a marker pen in and out of her mouth silently miming a blow job until she begins to laugh and ducks around the end of the aisle. When they finally give me the list, I find her and we go up through the maze of stairs and rooms, to the attic store. We climb into the gap between piled boxes of wallpaper and the cracked plaster of the ceiling.

Up here in the dusty warmth, the cocooning softness of the paper sucks in sound, keeps secrets. She tells me a lot of stuff when we hide. How she doesn't like her father, who isn't her father anyway, only her step-father. Although, she supposes, he's actually ok. How she likes to fuck her boyfriend on her father's desk and how he isn't a psycho like everyone says, just a bit of a dick sometimes, but just to be on the safe side I mustn't talk to her outside work, how she hates the town and the store and Burt and the others. Then, together, we plan how we'll leave; quit our jobs and go to a different town, better than this one. She will get a better job and I will be an artist. We'll share a flat and pretend we are in love.

Sometimes we kiss, both pretending it's just something we do to get through the tedium of the day. Today our boredom is acute. I open her coarse nylon shop coat and push it aside. We get as far as rubbing each other through our jeans before the noises we're making draw attention. Stella's silhouette appears at the door of the store room crooked with jealousy. When we feign innocence and go back to work I still haven't told her that there will be no more sneaking off, and there's no more time for planning.

Instead I go back out to where Wayne is working and tell him. He's quiet for a moment. He looks up as though I've betrayed him.

'So you off to be an artist then?'

'I'm off before this place traps me.' For some reason I find myself adding 'Did you know Burt painted pictures?'

'So that's why he likes you. Fuck. I knew there was something. I thought he just fancied you. You lying to wind me up?'

'Straight up. He told me so when I first came here.'

'Yeah, well, Hitler painted pictures too.'

At 6.56pm I've sold the day off cheaply for the last time. I stand at the back door, killing time with the others, with perks of the job jammed into every pocket. We make difficult conversation as we wait for Burt to release us into the glistening dark. He looks at his watch and smiles like a saint. There's no more work to be done and nothing to do but wait out the last few minutes of the day but he'd rather go straight to hell than let us out early. He wanders among the different huddles, grouped according to rank and department, like a benevolent shepherd among his flock, but gradually he approaches me. He must know I'm leaving by now. Eventually all news always travels on the sour-grape vine. He leans in, closer, closer, till I can smell his aftershave. He speaks to me quietly, the way you talk to a fellow conspirator:

'You could do well here, young man,' he chuckles, 'You might have my job one day, if you kept your nose clean.'

Claire is looking out of the window at the empty yard. She doesn't look at me and I wonder if she knows? I don't know why I didn't say something to her when we were alone. I meant to. Now it's too late. Her boyfriend, the one who isn't a psycho, will be waiting for her outside. Maybe I was afraid to find out that she would rather stay here after all.

The clock above the door counts down and we pretend not to watch it, all waiting for the moment the door's thrown open and we disperse into the surrounding streets hurrying away to bus stops and old bangers parked in back streets.

I stand outside for a moment and watch as Claire walks towards a car with blacked out windows. She pauses briefly and glances a goodbye before she disappears behind tinted glass.

Burt is behind me. I can smell his cheap cigs. 'I expect she'll miss you, even if nobody else will.'

I don't say anything and for a moment we stand together in the doorway.

'Did I ever tell you that I paint pictures, young man?'

'No, Burt. You never did.' I laugh because he's told me a dozen times. Even he smiles.

'They're not like you and me, the people 'round here. They don't understand.' He turns the lights off. 'Well, good luck young man.' He can barely bring himself to say it.

Marcus Smith

Daisy

Watch for predators, cars, angry streets.
The car hit the bicycle. The ambulance siren
and bombs. At school. On the bus. Restaurants.
In the airport when we go. Where we go.

I am a daisy losing my yellow petals,
and I am one big puff of white seeds
The wind blows away. I land in a garden,
a quiet one with walls and gates and guards

and there I forget our tall walls and gates
because the ivy grows, and the guards are outside
and I never go out. No one knows I'm here
in a garden. The ivy walls are invisible. I grow.

The Children Go For A Walk

We see Live Girls on walls and Bomb Attack,
fast cars and loud buses to watch out for.
A bird jumping from a tree doesn't fly back.

Lots of signs. *No* on the bars of a door.
Pictures of dead soldiers in the news rack,
litter stuck to the walls of the corner store.

We wait for Green Man in the traffic light.
A man bumping into my friend doesn't wait,
two ladies yell and swear and have a big fight

over a parking space. A puppy tries to break
his leash, tugging hard like my heart-shaped kite.
A snarling pitbull and his crazy owner make

us hurry back to school, where we must tell
Our teacher what she saw. She writes her story
by us on the board and doesn't always spell

all of our words ("bomb," "bar," "crazy")
or write how Crazy looked as bad as a smell.
So it's Green Man, green tree, happy puppy.

Who will I be when nothing bothers me?

Fugue with Her Ancestors

A wax carver from Russia, he rode a horse
    (She likes to watch a candle burn, burn down)
all the way to Hamburg and married a circus rider
    (but pities the one-track lives of trick horses)
whose son left for England and ended there as
    (blinkered as greyhounds chasing a metal hare)
a bookie, card-sharp and dog-racer
    (her father inventing pills long lives)
while she wonders why not travel elsewhere
    (and spent his end tallying great, great sums)
while she most fears becoming somebody
    (in his dirty bathrobe, every day the same)
while she changes her wardrobe as often as she can.

Gillian Penrose

The Rent Collector

If you passed him on Clyde Road
this man might well have a desk job.
When the rent for our student flat fell due
he arrived quietly, let himself in:
average height, thin with greying hair,
wearing a colourless gaberdine mac
but elegant glossy brown shoes.

Difficult to assign any sinister motives
though his manner was disconcerting,
especially when I was alone.
Without gesticulations and little conversation,
he jotted down transactions left-handed.

The limp white hands had long fingers
with Mandarin length nails
any woman would envy.
Always an unsettling moment
when handing over the money—
he took it in his right hand,
which had two thumbs.

Dunbeath

Here it is enough to find
a piece of mica on the beach,

see how it turns in the sun
to silver. As a child, you had the power

to transform everything. Broken glass
was precious cargo. Wise as the fool

who traded gold for withered apples,
you knew the names of things.

Enough to see a small brown
bird on a wet stone,

its leg as thin as wheat grass,
looking at you.

A single note half-taken by the wind
but your ear catches it. Is this the sign

that you have come so far to find
in the mid-day light—

thin strand of bird call,
watchful eye?

Sticks are for Fire
Zoe Gilbert

A cured stick for a stirrer. A sturdy one for a sweeper. Brittle sticks for tinder. A green branch to hang the pot. A forked one for ceremony.

I chose my sticks with wisdom. It were a green day, a bird sang I remember while I walked up. Unwound the ivy, careful, and noted the turn of the coil. Sunwise a good sign for a merry-weather stick, widdershins for doing the darks. Two forked sticks, among all those sticks that were mine. And then those small pink hands holding them, like mole paws before the skins are dried out. A mole paw is good for an earth curse, or to find the way in a moonless night. What moon is it tonight? My bones can't tell me. Cover my peepers and I can see most things, just ask me, but now I see nothing. Those were my sticks, in those small pink hands. They were my bones, my skull, my fingers, and those of them that'll waggle still I've walked about me and I've felt a bit of what the sticks have done. There's pulpy parts, sticky messes. What was wet has dried to crusts, mostly. Some fingers are stuck together with it. Eyes gummed tight shut. That's if there's still eyes, under these crackly lids.

'Who told you such a tale?' Shilla McVie rears up from the earth wild-eyed and brandishes her spade high in the air, sending a hail of soil over her two daughters. 'Who told you and how much?'

Bryony glares down at Gertrude, but she has on that mask she can conjure sometimes that makes her into a dolly, silent and with painted on eyes. Around their mother's feet lie stones and dandelion roots like witches' fingers, torn from the vegetable patch. Bryony thinks of mandrakes, their silent screams, and the screams that echoed in the story they have heard. She wants more; for the shadowy horrors to be brought out into the chilly light.

'It were Dandie,' she mumbles, 'We went for the eggs like you asked and he came along with his fiddle and...'

'It were Dandie.' Shilla McVie shoves the spade down into the clumpy earth at her feet where it splits a root with a crunch. She rubs her huge hands over her face, and when her arms drop down her features are changed. Her bulgy eyes look tired.

'That's folk for you,' says Shilla, eyeing the broken ground. Neither Bryony nor Gerturde make a sound, there's nothing at all but the daft cheeps from the nest in the wych elm and the hush-hush of its new leaves. Bryony bites on her thumb and thinks how her lips would feel if they were in that tale they'd heard, split and squishy as gone-over raspberries.

'Is it true, then?' asks Gertrude. Bryony wonders where she gets that stone inside her from, even though she's so small; how she can squash the fear like a frog under that stone that gets them both into such trouble.

Shilla squats down and takes a handful of soil, rubbing it between her fingers to test its goodness. 'It were a long time ago, so long now it don't matter so much, but it's a lesson for you meddlers in its way.'

'What's the lesson?' says Gertrude. Her black hair is sticking out in tufts from her bony head, and Bryony thinks of moss on a small boulder.

Shilla heaves herself upright and gazes at the girls. 'Spades and forks, the pair of you. Get your pinnies on and follow the furrow behind me.'

'Do you think she'll tell?' Bryony whispers to Gertrude as they carry the tools back to the garden.

'I'll make her tell,' says Gertrude. 'Don't you want to know?'

'I don't want a bruise for the school house tomorrow.'

'Don't be such a rabbit-bottom. It'll be worth it. And it were real people who lived here who did it, and a real witch.'

'Just keep that tongue of yours in your mouth if she gets uppity.'

Gertrude glares over her shoulder at Bryony as she marches up behind their Ma's wide haunches, bent double as she rips bramble roots from the earth.

'Tell us the story while we dig, Ma,' Gertrude says. 'We're eager for the lesson.'

Bryony gives her a shove that makes her stagger as they crouch and begin to turn the soil with their forks.

All those little faces, so close, I found that a strange thing. Little limbs that look so soft and harmless, at the distance their mammies tend to keep them. Little skipping feet and clapping hands. I think of them that way, or I did, when I thought of children. I'd no longing anymore for my own. I spelled that out of myself so many years ago I've forgot the feel of it. But there, they are all about, you cannot go without spotting them jinking here and there, jibber-jabbering like birdies. I see the life in them. I seen the big ones, half child half man, and the mischief they gets into, clobbering each other and howling up through the woods where they think nothing but rabbits spies them. But the bitty ones, who'd think they have that strength secret in their chickeny arms, who'd think there was anything but feathers in their wibble-wobble heads? I've the proof of it, here in these clotty wounds and these pulpy parts that might still be my eyes.

'Your father and me were as small then as the pair of you, and likely no better, but no worse neither. We learned our right and wrong in the school house, and my own Ma and Pa kept my back straight and my nose out of muck.' Shilla pauses to chuck a flint from the furrow and it chinks against the pile under the elm. 'Your father weren't so fortunate with his own family, scoundrels they were though I didn't know it then, but he weren't a bad boy. No, we might have been starved half stupid some years and freezed out of our wits every winter, but we knew good and bad. All the children did. That's what made it such a peculiar thing, what happened.'

Shilla McVie's face is as ruddy and broad as her red forearms, and just as hard-looking. Bryony can't shrink her Ma down to child height in her mind, with that bristly brow and her chin that sticks forward whenever she bellows—and it's usually a bellow—at her daughters. She tries to slice into the earth in the same rhythm as Shilla's spade, to keep from being noticed and halting the story, wishing Gertrude would do the same instead of toppling about.

'There were a woman then, lived up in one of the shieling houses all year round. Liked to be left alone, and with good reason they said.'

'What was her name?' says Gertrude, already huffing with the effort of turning the earth. She's only two years younger than Bryony but half the size, measly and sunken like the last batch bun that gets made up from a scrap of dough.

'When did your nose get so sharp?' Shilla turns and Bryony tries not to look up at the swollen blue eyes that fix on her sister, but Gertrude doesn't even slow at her digging.

'May. Old May.' Shilla returns to her spade and goes on, breathing deep. 'She had hair down to her knees that she wound up in grey knots around her ears like mouldy bannocks, and just enough teeth to get the flesh from a rabbit bone. She didn't come down near the other houses much, meaning people had a good stare when she did, and the children hid behind their mams like mice when a cat's about. Me and my brother were no better, peering out at her and whispering.'

'What did they say?' Gertrude manages between wheezes.

'The same nastiness you tiddly ones likely say about old Ma Scrall now. That she ate mice so she needn't come down to the village for her vittles. That she went about at night so as not to show that she had no shadow.'

Bryony shudders at the thought of Ma Scrall, and the top of her head that is as bald as an egg, with just a wisp of hair floating above it. She won't keep it covered, so you have to pretend you're not looking at it or you haven't noticed and while you try to think of something ordinary to say she looks right in through the fronts of your eyes and laughs at the real thought you're having, about her head like an egg.

'We were taught better than to say such things, but we knew she were different. People stopped their gabbing when she came near. She never were invited into a house like others, nor mentioned in prayers at church. That were one place she wouldn't go near at all.'

'Witches can't go in the church,' says Gertrude. She flicks soil up into the air with her fork. 'They turn to ash-dust if they cross the threshold. Piff paff!'

I heard them coming. Thought I'd slipped up and forgot a celebration day. They traipsed along, clanging and clacking. It's a procession I thought, going up to bless the shieling houses or some such. They are always on and on with their rituals, blessing this and blessing that. Shouts rang about, but nothing to prick my ear. Children's voices, little birdie squawks, they don't sound a thing to fear. I kept right on with my work. Just then it were tying up the new herbs into posies, to hang and dry. I think of them as posies, but where there'd be flowers there are the hints, the glints, of their powers. Shame I hadn't the time or the insight to use them then. A stronger one than me, a woman with the true sight, might have seen what was coming. I scratched the ashes with a stick, my forked stick for the purpose, and saw only a storm in the grate.

'Who said a word about a witch?' Shilla McVie swings round and Bryony shrinks back, bumping Gertrude with her elbows.

'Dandie did,' Gertrude replies, quick as a slap. 'He said she'd been up to mischief, upsetting folk. He didn't say what she'd done.' Bryony is watching her Ma too carefully to be able to give her sister a pinch. Shilla's wide red face switches between angry and sad and something else. Her eyebrows bristle. Bryony waits for a bellow, for a palm swinging her way, but instead her Ma turns and continues digging.

'Never mind what Old May were up to. It's too long ago to be sure of it, anyway. What's certain is that she got the wrong side of Sorrel Stott.'

The rhythm of Shilla's spade slicing into the ground goes on. Bryony can just hear the chicks peeping from the tree behind them, the tiny wheedling sounds, so pitiful. She thinks of mandrakes again, screams that happen only in your head. What sounds does a witch make when she is hit? Would it be a roar, or a dreadful squeal like a rabbit makes when its leg is caught in a trap?

Gertrude is poking her in the bum, hissing something or other about Sorrel Stott, but Bryony bats her hand away. She wants to keep the cold blood feeling that the scream in her head is making.

'That's where things went awry. Mark it, the pair of you. If somebody does you wrong, you sit back and ease your mind and puzzle a while over why they did so. If you can't make head nor tail of it, you puzzle a while longer and you keep on pondering until you run out of steam. You don't go with that boiling pot in your head and start scalding others with your own stew.'

Shilla's voice is turning crackly, like there's a leaf pile in her throat and her words have set it alight. Bryony tries to unthink her bad thought, that her Ma is hardly the one to be preaching about cooling down before taking trouble to a person. But this burn-hole in her Ma's fierceness is curious.

'That were Sorrel's failing, then. She boiled up and boiled up until she couldn't get quiet again. And she began talking, to any that would listen, and especially to the tiddlers because we'd swallow any old tell-tale story like it was. Her rage was like a new, shining thing to us. Something frightening, but you drink it up, like those ghoulish tales you hear in the bard house in winter. We listened, and with all those ears turned up at her, Sorrel's stories got wilder, and her rage became like a spell with all of us under it. We danced like empty-headed puppets for her, just to keep in the fiery heat of it, to feel the unnatural power of her rage coursing in us.'

Shilla's voice crackles so much that with a snap it seems to break, and Bryony watches her Ma take one heavy step away from the furrow and thump herself down on the heap of weed stalks beside them. She looks worn out, like all that talk of fire and rage has sucked the red out of her. She is staring at the furrow she has dug, her breathing still heavy from the work, but Bryony can tell that it is not soil she is seeing with her big round eyes.

Kelpie is mewing near me somewhere. Perhaps she has found her brother. I named him after a boy I knew, once, when I were a bitty one. Hunter. By name and by nature, for he brought me a catch each night, the rascal. I called for him then. My eyes were already blind with the blood but I could hear. Through all their hubbub of hollering and smashing there was the sound of his cry. Worse than the hurt I felt all through my bones was that cry. My mind turned then, for not being able to bear it. When I woke, it were all silent, just this mush of me left. I am spared the sight of my Hunter, but the mewing of his sister makes him slink through my head. She is licking my cheek, I feel the heat of her tongue, but how it stings. Like a lick from a nettle. Kind cat, kinder than folk. Don't mew. Lick these crusts from my eyes, let's see what's left of them.

Bryony has an urge then, to sit beside her Ma and lean on the hillock of her shoulder, but there is a kind of spell cast even now. Gertrude stands still beside her, trying to quiet her gusts of breath, watching the thunder pass through their Ma's face.

'We did her bidding. We followed the force of her will up the hill, so strong it was I believe our own souls were left behind. She wished Old May dead, did Sorrel Stott. And she got her way, with not a drop of blood on her hands.'

Shilla McVie sits, her eyes covered by her great, grimy fingers, and her daughters listen to the small green leaves of the wych elm, hush-hushing above them, and the tiny cheeps from the nest in its branches.

Their Ma speaks again, as if she hears the questions bursting in her daughters' mouths.

'Sticks, they used, that were laying about. Stones from the crumbling hill wall. There were such a number of us, mad with that woman's rage, we filled the shieling house like a starling storm. After, the place were so stained, in Old May's blood and her howls, and in the minds of all of us, that they burned it. Old May were still inside. No man checked for breath, for a stirring of life, before they piled up the sticks all round and put a flame to the thatch.'

The flutter of the green leaves turns to the licking of flames in the fast hill winds. The calls of the baby birds become the mewing of a lonely cat—for a witch always has a cat—as it watches its home become a bonfire. Bryony shudders again, seeing at the centre of the bonfire the messy, sticky bundle of Old May, clawing away the embers of thatch that drop onto her broken body. She feels a hard nudge from Gertrude, and as the smoke and flames clear from her eyes there is the shape of her Pa, stamping across the muddy ground towards them.

'What's this? Shilla? Girls, what troubles your mother?' There are little shakes running through Shilla's shoulders, her huge hands cover all of her face. Pa's shadow looms over her as his stare slides from one daughter to the other. 'What have you done, you weasels?' He lunges towards them, Gertrude swerves and he grabs Bryony by the scruff of her neck, snagging her skin so she gasps. She feels her feet lift off the ground, the fork drop from her fingers.

'Let her down.' Shilla's voice comes out soggy, snuffly. 'It's my doing, they've done nothing but listen.' Bryony stumbles as her feet touch the ground and she falls into the furrow, soil gritting her cheek.

'Listen? To what?' asks her Pa.

'They heard a snippet today of what became of May Mort. I told them the rest, by way of a lesson.'

'You told them. All of it?'

'The parts that matter.'

'They're not the only ones wants a lesson.' Her Pa's boots step right over Bryony and she peers up from the furrow just in time to see her Ma's head sent flicking to one side by the clout of his fist.

'That tale's not for the ears of anyone living, least of all our own daughters.' His fist strikes Shilla's head back the other way, and her body slumps after it so that she lies on the ground. 'Not for nobody, ever. You learn that lesson and you keep it, Shilla.' As his boots thud away, Shilla's blue eyes meet Bryony's across the broken earth. Bryony stares, and for a moment it is like looking into her own eyes, like seeing another girl just like her. The girl is afraid, even more than Bryony, but most of all she is ashamed.

Bryony can't bear to look then. She closes her eyes, and listens to the tree, to its flickering leaves and the sad, sad sound of the lonely witch's cat.

Patricia Wooldridge

Knit Forward, Purl Back

A life of all our jumpers, baby clothes, Dad's cardigans
to four rows at the day centre, a bag with your name on,
telling me how the ladies revolt, refuse and stop—
all we do is sit and knit, we don't know why or who for—

one casts hers off and says it'll do as a floor cloth.
You're at the back, doing your rows — it passes the time
until lunch. And here, tucked in my drawer, your hand-
knitted tea-cosy, in even stripes, never a mistake.

The stocking stitch chat of needles, the stroke of wool
winding through your fingers, catching up on the tick
of the clock at home, the rhythm of unshared thinking,
broken in a glance — outside your window — there

a painted bird you've never seen, hopping on the lawn.
Reaching for the phone, you ask me — such a pink-brown,
black and white with a check splash of blue —
huge beside the sparrow.

A jay in your garden, the forest builder, alarm caller
through the shadows of our bluebell wood,
where we always strolled and I picked drooping stems
for your kitchen sill, an acorn flight from our door.

Reading the Lake

Today the lake
is full of triangles,

diagonal wind
tearing the clouds;

a lull in the rain
to fit the hour I had

away from the gift
of a warm flannel

to my mother's face,
never opening her eyes,

to wander the waterlogged heath,
sit and note:

the grebes are sprouting
their spring head ruffs.

Song in E Minor

The owl we bury here, by the shooting
bluebells, and the mistle tempers
his three note song, high overhead—

a minor key of softened warble—how
beginnings will begin and feed
this hunger of living,

her death cradled in my hands—still warm—
her broken neck—too low—too late—scooping
from the middle of the lane in my ungloved
hands—such tawniness—stroking.

The mistle thrush clear on the tip
of bare poplar, speckled breast catching the sun,
his trig point song, calling.

Coop
Emma Greenwood

'Mum! Mum? Can I pull the radishes?'

Saffy's shouting from the top of the garden and I'm washing up in the kitchen. Sunshine's streaming through the open window and a fat bumblebee's blundering against the glass trying to escape.

Saffy doesn't like radishes. Correction. She *does* like radishes: she likes their quick growing-cycle; she likes their pink skin and mousey white tails; she likes putting seeds in the earth and watching them sprout; but she doesn't like eating them.

Matt's away.

If I let her pull them, it'll be me eating their spicy white flesh all week.

I hurry to the kitchen door, my hands dripping with suds.

'You can pull five. Just *five*.' I hold up a sopping hand—my fingers stretched out, one for each radish.

Saffy squints at me from our unruly veg patch. She's got a bucket in her hand. I see radish leaves spilling over the rim.

'Have you pulled them already?' I ask.

Saffy slips the bucket behind the hedge and picks up a trowel. She doesn't look at me. 'Just doing some digging,' she says.

I sigh and turn back to the kitchen wondering if Steve across the road has a thing for radish.

Matt comes home on Friday night. On Saturday, I offer him radishes—Steve declined with a smile.

Matt looks at their shrivelled skins and soft bodies and shakes his head.

'I'm not hungry,' he says and pushes his chair back. 'And I'm meeting Paul for a curry later.'

Saffy looks down at the table.

I take six radishes from the dish and lay them on my plate.

'Are you sure you won't try one?' I ask her.

She pulls a face. 'No way!'

On Sunday, Matt sleeps till noon. I sit on the edge of the bed and shake him gently.

'Lunch in half an hour,' I say.

He groans and pulls the duvet over his head. Through the open window, I hear Saffy talking to the courgettes she's just discovered amongst the veg patch brambles. 'Hello you!' she's saying.

'I'm leaving early today,' Matt mutters. 'Flight's at four. Won't need lunch.'

I'll have to say it now, then.

'Matt?' I say.

Matt groans again.

'I want to get chickens.'

Now the duvet's off and he's squinting up at me. There's sleep in the corner of one eye and a pillow crease down his cheek.

'You *what*?'

His breath smells of garlic and last night's wine.

'Chickens, Matt. You heard.'

'You can barely keep the house clean.'

'You only need two or three to get enough eggs—'

'You haven't told Saffy?'

'No.'

'Well don't. Look at your veg patch.' He shakes his head like I'm stupid. 'It's out of the question.' Then he picks up his phone from the bedside table and checks the time.

'Right,' he says. 'I've got thirty minutes. Wake me up at one.'

The next week we're eating courgettes. I make stir fry and soup and slice them on pizza and grate them into omelettes. Omelettes from supermarket eggs. Matt doesn't like courgette, but that doesn't matter because Matt's not here.

At the weekend, I go to Mum and Dad's cottage.

Matt stays at home to work.

'Matt won't let me have chickens,' I say to Mum. We're sat at the kitchen table, the table where I, aged six, dipped soldiers into bright yolked eggs that came still warm from next door's coop. The table where Matt proposed to me one midsummer's morning, seven years ago, after staying up to see in the dawn.

Mum sips her tea.

'Well it's not like you've got the time, have you?'

I suppress the urge to smash my cup on the floor.

'You don't have to bottle-feed them every three hours for goodness sake!' I glug back my tea. 'Where's Saffy? I need a walk.'

'She's out back with your father, chopping wood.'

As she speaks, Saffy bursts in through the door, arms stacked with firewood. I count her fingers—just to check—and breathe a sigh of relief that Matt's not here to see her play lumberjack.

We go out, across the road, over the gate into the field, and follow a barbed wire fence caught with dirty sheep wool and shreds of old feedbags, down to the river. The air smells of manure and across the fields a tractor grumbles along the Machynlleth Road. Dad walks ahead, like he always does, hands in pockets, head down. Saffy runs behind trying to keep up with him.

'So you serious about those chickens?' Mum asks falling into step with me. We turn away from the fence and cross the field towards the river.

I think about the washing pile, the ironing, the un-mown grass, the school run, Saffy, the brambles in the veg patch, the business I want to start. 'I don't know.'

'We had chickens once,' Mum says. 'Do you remember?'

I shook my head. 'No.'

'We'd not had them long before your father got rid. Scratched up his lettuce, they did.'

Chickens in Dad's regimented rows!

'Marcie says if you keep them in the…'

'Saffy, NO!'

I break off and dash towards the river. Dad's holding Saffy over the edge of the bank to look at something.

'Get away from the edge, Dad!'

'Quiet!' he hisses back.

'Granddad's found a burrow,' Saffy looks over her shoulder at me and grins, but I grab her arm and pull her away.

'Mum!' she protests and shakes me off.

Dad ignores us. He watches the riverbank. Then he looks up at a tiny dot mewing high in the sky above, mutters 'Buzzard', and takes off across the field scattering sheep in his wake. We follow, like we always do, Dad choosing our route, no consultation.

On Sunday, we get home just as Matt's leaving.

'Daddy!' shouts Saffy throwing open the car door and flinging herself across the pavement at Matt.

'Careful,' Matt says, backing off. 'New suit.'

He brushes the spot where Saffy grabbed him.

'Are you going already?' she asks, and then, without waiting for an answer. 'Guess what Grandad gave us?'

Matt points his key-fob at his car. The indicators flash. He opens the door and lays his bag on the passenger seat.

'I have no idea,' he says.

'Mummy,' Saffy calls. 'Can I show Daddy what Grandad gave us?'

I reach over to the back seat and get the bag.

'Radishes!' Saffy shouts dragging it from my hand. 'Gran says they've got too many!'

Later, when Saffy's in bed, I go on the internet and order a coop. I order two bags of feed, three bags of bedding and a run. Then I settle back with a cup of tea and browse chickens.

Annie Bien

Four Corners

Snow carves leaf veins
upon mountains,
glacial sweeps sprinkle
confections of white
shadowed blue
by passing cloud flotillas.

Contrails streak the morning sky.
A metal wing cuts a hawk's path
lower than Icarus:

Once my brother dreamed of flying
then his feathers began to melt.
He upgraded, and reprogrammed,
rebooted his ears, readjusted
his webcrawling thoughts
to a twenty-four hour feed.
His blood pools then backs up
into inkblotches.
He pulls down the cyber shutters
annoyed by the sun.

The rivers and gullies
ink serpentine runes.
Wending and weaving,
the water buoys
our bodies,
not discriminating
friend or foe.

The Sweeper

He sits on cardboard, broom against the wall.
Passers-by step around him, looking but don't see.

Taxis and delivery trucks honk and squeeze
down the Chinatown street, mixing soysauce and diesel.

He begins to sweep cigarette butts, wrappers,
five-spice chicken wing—sweep sweep—dustpan

sweep sweep—drop in bin. Students push by
the sweeper with head bowed low—

they've heard that the guru is magnificent,
he escaped Tibet, one of the last greats, renown

friend of the Dalai Lama. One wrinkles her nose—
rotting leftover takeout, not a rat was that, urine—

another shust the door in the custodian's face—
two press together, name dropping great lamas,

great gurus, great blessings. A new student opens
the door for the sweeper.

In the temple, a hush of anticipation—will the guru
be clad in gold brocade, enter with his entourage

like in the Land of Snows? Will he have attendants?
What will it be like to be his student? The little hand clicks

on the hour of seven. The translator walks through the doorway,
all the students rise for the grand lama, hands together.

He enters, clad in denim shirt and jeans. The sweeper
waves his hand. *Please sit. Have seat. I'm very pleased to see you here.*

Jane McLaughlin

Greenwich Time

Time clumps so thick here
you can put your hand on it
where tourists queue in rain
to stand one foot either side
of the zero meridian.

It's channelled across the ceiling
in sparking green laser. Outside it clunks
pinball fashion off the observatory domes.
Lightning spears the park below,
the thunder-time measuring distance.

No truck here with those
who say it doesn't exist, runs backwards
or sideways. You can feel it push
in your step on the path, heartbeat,
the drum of rain on the lead roof.

The red ball rises, falls, on its tower
at one o' clock. It gave time
to those who had no clocks
sent time out to the river, to ships
that could at least know when they started.

In the quiet monastic rooms
the astronomers did hand-to-hand combat
with the universe, night after night
measuring, recording the myriad working
of the cosmic clock.

Flamsteed did thirty thousand
observations. Until he had it in all
its wayward precision.
The place throngs with clocks, chronometers,
sundials, beating and keeping time.

Downstairs, three great clocks
sail like brass galleons into the future,
round weights rocking on their arms.
And one big watch. The last, right answer.
Round and perfect as the moon.

EXtreme Deep Field

EXtreme
X is what we do not know
but may know us, seeing though
tissue and blood to the naked bone.
The constellation Fornax (furnace)
is where they find XDF
2.3 arcminutes by 2 arcminutes.
Astronomers measure it
as if it were curtain material
but its farthest light
came forth only 450 million years
after the Big Bang.

Deep
Hubble stared for ten years
with its Cyclops eye
at one small dark patch,
snaring it with eight wavelengths,
the longest twice that
of the reddest red we can see
or imagine.

Field
It has the name of meadow, grazing, grass.
It blooms with orange and blue flowers
scattered haphazard
like the pretty weeds
either side of the back lane.

After Woolwich

Nine hundred and forty-three steps
from my house to the station.
This morning at the curve of the road
I have gone four hundred and twenty.
A tall thick-set black man comes towards me
holding a small boy by the hand.

The boy is wearing enormous sunglasses
with fluorescent yellow frames.
It is raining, a thin mean rain.

'Too much sun.' I say as they pass.
The man laughs, a big chunky laugh,
and we go on in our different directions.

I could have run after them, I could have said:
'They can't make us hate each other.'

Since not far away the flowers pile in the street
it does not need saying.

And without laughter we are all lost.

Slag

Tracey Iceton

They calls me a slag, see. Curse me for it, they do, as they pile me up, swell my huge bulk, grow me day by day. They should be giving me my proper name, call me what I am; a spoil tip, a pit heap, a gob pile. I'm the coal board's whore, it's true, but slag I am not. I'm shale and rocks and rubble, I am, all built on sweet Welsh sandstone and fresh mountain springs. I'm their pride and joy, a towering monument to the lives sacrificed underground for their precious black gold. And here I stand, mistress of the valleys, hundreds of feet tall, widest at my base and tapering to my conical crown. They think I rule this land, merciful and benign. But kind I isn't. My heart's afire, there's a heat in my belly and I'm burning, see, from the inside out. They thinks they can treat me like a whore; here when they needs me, ignored when they don't. If it's for a whore they wants me they'll have to pay the price, see.

Her belly's bad this morning. It's been bad for a while but it's extra bad today. She can feel it, even lying still as a stone, on her narrow bed with the blankets swaddling her. There's a monster inside her, trying to beat its way out, a chick cracking through an egg, fierce with life. She puts her hands on her belly. Pushes down, trying to keep the pain inside, hold the skin together. Stop the monster from breaking the surface of her eggshell stomach.

Downstairs her mam calls.

'Lillian, it's late. Get dressed.'

At least under the loose, baggy cardy and too-big blazer of her uniform the monster is hidden. She throws back the covers.

'I'm coming now, in a minute.'

Her monster bucks and writhes. She struggles to sit, stand, walk. The hook-and-eye fastener on her skirt won't close its mouth. She loops an elastic band, uses a safety pin, keeps everything held together.

In the kitchen her mam and tad are talking.

'It's not right, see. A girl her age shouldn't be going out nights.'

'It's only with her friends. What's the harm?'

'The harm's those boys, isn't it. With their long hair and their flappy trousers. I don't like it, see.'

'Davy, hush, that's your own daughter you're speaking ill of.'

'You know what trouble's to come from boys the like of them.

Turning my daughter into a slut, that's what they'll be after.'

In the passageway, deep inside her, the monster hears her tad's words. Outraged, it riots, coiling and twisting like it would be out of her, through the door and round her tad's throat, squeezing the life from him. She tries to console it with gentle strokes. But it won't be quieted this morning. She takes her duffle coat from the peg. Does up the toggles, all but the last which can't stretch to its partner hole. Her satchel lies by the door. The homework she didn't do is crinkled at the bottom of it. Last night the monster wouldn't let her get on.

'Lillian, are you not having some breakfast?' her mam asks.

'I'll have some at school.' She shoulders her bag, keeps her back to her mam.

'Well, are you coming home straight after, tonight?'

She looks back, twisting her head, feeling the stretch all the way down to her strung-tight belly.

'I'm away out.'

'Where to?'

'A friend's. To study.' And she's gone, out the door and into the low-slung grey that shrouds the village's terraced streets this morning.

When first they birthed me I was bach like a molehill. A few lorry loads, that first day, was all it took, isn't it, and I was born. I didn't know then what their plans for me were. I thought I was a molehill; creatures all blackened with earthy dirt, blinking in the light their poor eyes wasn't used to seeing, had made me, burrowed me out from my underground womb. And happy I was to be out, see. In the sunlight, the free flowing air. Breathe, I could. Didn't I enjoy that, and the view, which wasn't much compared to my grand-high vista now. But I had colours for the first time; greens, blues, yellows, reds: whites. It was a kaleidoscope feast after my diet of black, isn't it. The cold I didn't enjoy so much. I was sired in heat and ripped out from it. The hillside was nithering; die I thought I would. I cursed the evil that brought me to the surface. But my blinking, blackened boyos were back the next day with more of me and once they built me up a way making my own heat, wasn't I. One thing I've never gotten used to, though, is all this rain. A right downpour we've been having and they don't care for me up here, getting the worst of it. I can feel it now, running all through me, tearing my skin loose, sliding whole parts of me away down the valley. I'm not happy to be out anymore, see. Taken all I can, I have.

She stands on the corner, gripping rough brickwork with thin, white fingers contracted tight. Her monster trying to kill her. She can't take a single step. Daren't move any part of herself for fear she'll split open like a rotten plum. She's afraid someone will see her standing there, pressed so hard to the gable wall she could hold up the entire row. She's afraid no one will see her standing there, her grey skirt, khaki coat, all washed and blurred by the fog. No one will come to help her.

Her pain sinks back down. The monster has worn itself out fighting her. She hurries, along the road, away from her school, to where she hopes there'll be help.

His mam opens the door.

'Hello, Mrs Davies, is Gareth here?'

His mam inspects her over brawny arms crossed and resting on a bosom that fed five little 'uns.

'He's gone to work this morning, just now.'

She's been left to it. The monster lashes out. She wrestles with the agony that ripples up from her belly, trying to halt it before it reaches her face.

'Lillian, is you alright?'

'Yes, Mrs Davies.' She turns. Hobbles down the street. No more questions, no more looking. She mustn't do anything else to anger the monster. It's going to kill her, she's sure, but maybe if she's nice to it, it'll kill her kindly.

Cars passing her on the road see only a hunched, dark figure curled around itself and wrapped in fog. The bus won't come for another hour. She's glad the fog hides her so well. They can't see her; she can't see them. There's nothing outside her except the greyness. Everything that matters is inside; memories in her head, passions in her heart, throbbings in her belly:

—Gareth, we mustn't, see. You'll get me into bother, isn't it.

—Lillian, my Lillian, I loves you.

She checks her watch. Still three quarters until the bus. She should be in geography, reading her books on mountains, earthquakes, landslides, trying to write up her homework under the desk without Mr Evans seeing.

The monster has been hushed for a while. Maybe it's sleeping. She closes her eyes. In and out, she drifts, flying over mountains, soaring and diving through clouds, hovering over the valleys. Not valleys, one valley. Her valley. She can see it bright and sharp; the tiny pock-mark of the village, brown and flecky, against the green of the hills and, high up to the west, one black gash glowering down on them: the slag heap. In her dream it shimmers like thick, dark oil, undulating and flickering. Alive. She can feel it pouring over her in silky warm waves.

A horn beeps. The bus. She leaps up. Feels the gush between her legs, silky warm waves.

Here they comes, my dark-crusty boyos. In their lorries they come to dump their loads on me, over me: into me. Their rubbish, that's all I am, and pregnant with it now, heavy and laden. I'm ready to breach, see. Out of me it's coming, slipping and sliding, running backwards downhill. Outgrown this hillside, haven't I? So it's time I put their tidy venture to my back, shows the coal board a cold shoulder, press my weight against it, see. Push myself out of me. I can't be staying up here. The ground beneath me is too weak for the giant they've made me. I've tired, I have, of their playing at families, raising me up from their cast-off. Away back where to I came from, that's the place for me now, see. Run there as fast as I can, I will. Taking all four hundred thousand tonnes of me, all my billions of shalestone off-spring. My labour will be my death, isn't it. But I'll die feasting on my beautiful valley, see.

The bus to her nain and taid's climbs out of the village. The road winds tight and slow up to the east. She knows it will take a long time to get there. She knows it will be too long and balls her hands into fists. She would pound the monster with those tiny, clenched weapons, if only she thought she would win.

Inside of her, the monster is impatient. It wriggles around, looking for an escape. The weight of it surges forwards and downwards, towards red light. She feels the coming. Knows there is no way to stop it, hold it back. It will be born. Pain screams from her mouth. The world screams back, a roar ripped from the land of her childhood.

The bus stops. People turn, point. Add their screams to hers. Think her scream is like theirs. She strains herself, her whole tiny body flexing, expanding, contracting. Squeezing the monster out of her, repelling it like fatal waste.

'Please help,' she gasps to the lady beside her.

But the lady only stares out the window. She stretches a useless hand, the other crams itself into her mouth, hiding from horror. Lillian, wallowing in herself, cranes her neck, fills her rolling wet eyes with the grimy pane. Outside, away to the west, she sees it now, moving, sliding. Racing towards the village. Bearing down on them all. The slag heap. The one she used to play on with her butties, when they were bach. The one that has grown larger than the god-made mountains. It engulfs the village, submerging homes, the school, the classroom, the desk. The chair that is empty because the monster in her belly wouldn't be quieted that morning. From their hillside view, all the passengers can do is watch the waves, black, slick, deep, as they slit the village, gutting it like the doctor's knife.

'Please, oh God, please.' Lillian stretches a hand with the last of her own free will. Tugs at the lady's sleeve. 'It's coming.' She points to her belly, the blood pooling on the seat between her legs, gushing onto the floor.

The lady sees now. Springs up. Speaks words that wash over Lillian, lost in her pain as the monster tears her flesh apart with angry, striving fists. She closes her eyes. Roars out, voice raised in chorus with the slag-slide on the hill. Feels the pop. A balloon pricked, deflated.

There, there. On her chest. In her arms. Red. Tiny. Crying. Reaching out to take hold of her, suckle. Her shiny new daughter.

They shouldn't have called me a slag, see. They should have shown me respect. Treasured me, to have and to hold, not dumped on me. Forgot, they did, that I was big enough to crush them all. Never again won't they treat me that way. My price is too steep, see.

This story is inspired by (but not based on) the 1966 Aberfan disaster when a mining spoil tip collapsed, sending 40,000 m^3 of debris down onto the Welsh village of Aberfan. The disaster destroyed the local primary school and resulted in the deaths of 144 people, including 116 children.

Aisling Tempany

Lines

Should I start with something metaphorical?
A childhood memory, something symbolic that would resonate with others.

Should I keep the lines short and neat
to punctuate those feelings more sincerely?
Why?
What difference does it makes where I break the line? Wouldn't the meaning be the same? Regardless of the rhythm and accuracy of the grammar, won't I still be sad? No matter where the sentence starts, you'll still be dead.

In the Kylemore Café, Dublin.

North-north-east of history
The revolving door spins through the present
Scrambled egg, bacon, white pudding,
Sky News and the latest British disgrace.
Prams, shopping, old ladies chewing their toast
The morning newspapers and sugar sachets
mixing with the splashes of milk,

before tables clear and fill again
with Chinese students, toddlers climbing
for paper cups of Coke.
A moment's silence is briefly heard,
before the cutlery clacks down
the chairs scrape, and a silent cloth
cleans the day away.

Rebecca Parfitt

Stitches

I'm unpicking the stitches you sewed
as I lay under you, your fingers fine as needles
fraying my skin, embedding yourself inside.

I find pieces of you I'd forgotten I carried,
pieces I can't remove.
I want to turn myself inside out and slowly,
unwind the thread, let the trail fall behind me
as you follow

but I'll be gone when you turn the corner,
just a snag of my dress caught on a bramble
and the blood of berries left crushed on the road,
replacing the heart you once held in your hands.

Sleepwalking

I return to you each time,
each time, a little further,
edging closer in,
returning to the beach
as the sea breathes long and hard,
pounding up and down the pebbles.

This was where you split me in half,
pitted the core,
then discarded it like a stone,
never looking back
to see the ripples in the water
spread their rings around you.

Sister

Stirs to reach out
from the edge of sleep.

She touches my arm,
gently clasps it,
checking I'm still there
before sliding back
to her sequence of dreams.

I wake as a line of wintry light
squeezes through the curtain,
forgetting she's not there
but asleep in another town.

The early morning shadows
mark the space of absence
and a crease in the sheets
folds over an imprint of her body,
left behind.

The Magnifico

Gina Challen

Nigel glanced through his windscreen at the building: neat red brickwork and green doors. He hated these church hall gigs but today would be different. A 'new start' with brand new material. In spite of what Sharon said, he was going to do his Big Trick. Right at the end. His *grand finale*. With all the practising, he knew he'd mastered it. Got it down to a fine art. It would put him up there with the best, and earn him a bit more money. Nigel took a quick drink from a plastic water bottle hidden in the inside pocket of his jacket. The cheap vodka burnt the back of his throat. He must remember to leave on time, Sharon was so set on these sessions they'd started going to: *helping couples to make relationships work better*. He snatched another mouthful and replaced the bottle.

He left his van and walked towards the hall. Glancing around, he spat his chewing gum under the boundary hedge, and turned the big metal ring to open the doors. Their resistance freed without warning, propelling him forward, and the resounding slam behind him announced his arrival. He put out a hand to steady himself against the wall, knocking against a laminated notice: *Please, Close the Doors Carefully*. It slid to the floor, landed print side down, and with a gentle sigh, spun across the tiled entrance way. He kicked the notice under the coat rail and stepped into the hall. Nothing was spoiling today.

At the front of the stage two young women were fixing a string of black and yellow bunting. The metallic tapping of their hammers against the heads of drawing pins masking their chatter. They stood back to admire the effect of their handiwork. Each triangle was appliquéd with a letter in alternate colours. Black on yellow. Yellow on black. *HAPPY BIRTHDAY BENEDICT*. They laughed and hugged their slender arms tight around each other. As they turned, the taller of the two moved forwards, her soft leather pumps making no noise on the wooden floor. Nigel was aware of a subtle scent as she stretched out her hand towards him. Light and floral.

'You're the Balloon Man? Hi. Poppy. I've set you up here. Yes?' She swung her arm wide, indicating the floor in front of the stage.

'The Magnifico...I'm The Magnifico. It's best if I'm on stage.

You know, for the act.'

Poppy stepped backwards, nose wrinkling. 'I thought you were a balloon man. Animals and hats. That sort of thing. I spoke to your wife. That's what she said. We agreed. I thought, perhaps you could just make things. For the children to take home. Okay? Best if you're down here. Better for the children. Yes?'

Nigel watched her hips sway as she walked towards the kitchen, blond ponytail bobbing.

Animals and hats. Christ! The Magnifico was better than that. They'd all agree about that by the end. And Sharon, booking kids' parties. This would be the last of those once word got around. Business cards. He'd get some new ones printed. Nice ones. Nigel dragged a table across the floor, the metal legs left scratches in the varnish, pale wounds across the wood. As usual there was no one to help him set up. Never mind, that wasn't going to upset him, not when he needed to concentrate on the big trick. He could hear laughter and women's voices. Odd snatches of sound as the kitchen door swung open, the rustle of cardboard and paper, the clinking of china. He heard Poppy say, 'Wait till you see what he's wearing. Polka dot bow-tie and striped jacket. Very end-of-the-pier.' There was laughter as the door closed. He'd told Sharon about the clothes but she insisted they helped him *get into character.* If today went to plan, it would be designer clothes from now on.

Birthday guests began to pack the carpark, children swinging and twisting from adult hands like bright little yoyos, crowding the hall entrance as their coats and hats were removed. Nigel, carrying his box in both hands, had to dodge parental elbows and small heads.

'Is that him? The balloon man, Daddy?' piped one small boy. Everyone turned to look as Nigel shoved through the crowd, a smile fixed to his face.

The hall filled. Children ran about shrieking, their feet drumming on the floor. Poppy appeared from the kitchen. At his table, Nigel concentrated hard as he laid out balloons in lines according to colour and shape. Sharon's idea. Red, blue, brown, green and white round, red, blue, green, brown and white long. They were slippery and wouldn't lie flat, a few dropped on the floor. The room slewed as he tried to pick them up and he put out a hand to steady himself. Nigel decided to leave them. Rummaging through the box, the sticky edge of a post-it note caught on his hand. Sharon's handwriting: *Don't do The Trick. You're not ready. Love you. S xx*

Music was turned on, the words of the song lost amongst the happy chaos. A dad started to dance, waving his arms above his head and swivelling his hips. He was joined by two young women and a small girl, amid noisy cheering from the other dads. Nigel looked at his watch. He was booked to start at four, it was now ten past. That was their problem. He'd cut the first part short. Tough. Six o'clock and he was out of here. He lifted a large electric pump and a tangle of flex from his box and set them on the table. Over the top of the pump, elevating it from the rest, Nigel laid an extra large red latex balloon. He ran his finger over it. Twenty quid was expensive, but it was worth every penny.

Eventually, Poppy rapped a spoon hard against the stage. Conversations stopped and someone turned off the music. The children gathered in front of Nigel, drawn by adult promises of balloon magic. They settled cross legged on the floor, their faces now serious. It was like story time at school. But better.

'Lovely to see everyone here, for Benedict's party. We're going to have a fun time with Mr Magnificent, The Balloon Man.' And she began clapping.

At bloody last! According to the clock on the wall it was twenty past four.

Nigel stepped forward, opened his arms wide with an extravagant sweep and bowed deeply. 'The Magnifico is here for your erudition and entertainment.'

Someone at the back of the hall sniggered, and was shushed. A couple of the children fidgeted. Nigel put a balloon to his mouth and started to blow. He blew up three long brown balloons, knotted the ends carefully and placed two of them on the table. He couldn't be bothered to talk, none of the usual, *who can guess what I'm making?* The third squealed and screeched as he twisted it to form a head at one end and a tail at the other. His head felt sore from the noise, as if it was being stung inside. He just twisted and turned the other two to make uneven legs.

'Here.' Nigel offered it to a girl in the front row. She looked at him with serious eyes as he dropped the balloon animal into her lap.

Next he made a yellow flower. Then a hat with a bobbing stalk. For twenty minutes he made balloon models, dropping them into the laps of the children. He made a blue and red giraffe and when it was finished Nigel looked round. Rocking slightly, he lent forward to a boy dressed as Batman.

'Here you, what's your name?' he asked, pointing the giraffe at the boy.

'Batman.'

'Your real name.' Nigel stepped in closer.

Before the child could reply, Poppy placed her hand on the small caped shoulder and said, 'Tea time, darling. Go and get some food.'

In the background, a woman called out, 'Time for tea everyone!' and the children were shepherded into another room. The boy remained at his mother's side. Someone had turned the music on again. Dancing feet thudded. The balloons on the floor skittered in the vibrations.

'You can't speak to him like that! We're having tea now. It's early but the children are bored. You're just not engaging with them. You see that, don't you? Let's try again after tea?'

'I don't like him, Mummy,' said Batman and, crossing one black booted foot in front of the other, he rose onto his toes and swirled off towards the cake.

Nigel's hands balled into fists and he pushed them inside his pockets. Bloody horrible kid. No manners. He should walk out. Leave them without any entertainment. That'd teach them. He turned back towards the table, felt in his box for his water bottle and tucked it in his pocket.

In the entrance Nigel pushed through the door marked *Gentlemen.* His face looked flushed in the mirror above the basins. He felt for the water bottle and pulled it free. Shaking he unscrewed the cap, threw back his head and shut his eyes. Leaning against the cold edge of the wash basin, he swallowed two big mouthfuls. Above his head, stuck firmly on the mirror, a sign urged, *Now please wash your hands.* No, he would go back. The Magnifico was nothing if not professional. They'd soon change their tune.

Nigel strode back into the hall. His legs felt wobbly and his head a little fuzzy, but that was to be expected before the Big Trick. Stage fright was good, it gave an edge to a performance, something Sharon could never understand. Poppy clapped her hands and the music was turned off. 'Let's all sit down for the next part of the show,' she said. A few children sat on the floor facing the table with Batman right at the front. His cape was pushed back and the emblem on his chest looked at Nigel as directly as a camera lens. The rest settled down by the adults, sitting on their laps or tucked in against their legs.

This was it. Nigel took a deep breath, selected the large red latex balloon, and with wave of his hand he turned on the pump. Everyone jumped. The immediate rush of air from the nozzle was as loud as a dozen vacuum cleaners. A couple of adults giggled and one child, lip tremulous, shuffled backwards on his bottom to his mother. The Magnifico fitted the balloon to the pump. He held the neck tight to the nozzle with his right hand, using the left, in showman style, to indicate its rapid growth.

When it swelled to over five feet in diameter, The Magnifico flicked the pump off and with a flourish pulled the balloon free, twisting the neck to stop the air escaping. The hall was silent. Latex whispered against the wooden floor, keeping time with the breathing of the audience. The Magnifico, lifted the balloon high, gave a small bow, and with one movement he pushed the neck inside the balloon, swiftly followed by his head. His face looked out through the red rubber, nose flattened against the side. The balloon bobbed and swayed, the latex as taut as the skin on a boil. Children shrieked. When some backed away their parents darted forward to pluck them from the shifting group. Everyone was watching now.

The Magnifico was centre stage at last.

Sliding both hands up inside the balloon, one each side of his face, and with a mixture of shoulder rolls and judicious tugging, he worked more of his body inside the balloon. As long as he kept the neck of the balloon tucked inside and tight against his body, no air could escape. The Magnifico had become a giant stopper. It was a struggle and as he jerked backwards and forwards he thought that he should have removed his jacket. He'd remember that for his future performances.

The Magnifico kept on twisting and turning. Every time he'd practised he'd been surprised by the small static shocks inside the balloon causing the hairs on his cheeks to stand up and stretch out towards the taut membrane. Right now he was sure the static was stronger, as if it were pulling at his whole body. He might fall forward at any moment. Almost there, he only needed to pull his feet free and secure the neck inside the balloon with a rubber tie.

Triumph. He was in, completely contained by the giant red balloon. The Magnifico strode across the floor, enclosed by the rubber, the tight red skin rolling along all around him. He smiled and waved from inside. Batman waved back. The Magnifico waved again. What did Sharon know? He was ready. It was all going well, the children loved him. He was *engaging*. He waved again, rolled to a stop in front of the children, and then Nigel realised he had no idea what he should do next. His stomach churned as he tried to remember. He was sure there was something else, he shouldn't be waving this much. What did the instructions say? Nigel felt vague and far away, he wondered if this were like drowning without any water.

He should've brought that book, he'd told her that, but Sharon hadn't listened. Too busy making them appointments to attend, *workshops for people at important relationship life stages*. Got it! Nigel remembered. Using his hands on the inside of the skin and shuffling his feet like a crab pulling itself from a rock pool, The Magnifico rotated the balloon until the neck was positioned above his head. With all of his body still encased, he undid the rubber tie, pushed his hands free through the gap of the neck, and wiggled his fingers. The Magnifico had made the massive red balloon grow hands. The children laughed and screamed. One small girl buried her face in her mother's lap. The act was going well, but The Magnifico was getting dizzy, it was time for him to emerge.

He placed his head under his wrists and pushed upwards. A small hiss of air escaped, stale with sweat, and his head popped out between his waggling hands. The Magnifico grinned down at the children, his vast round body topped with a grimacing face and framed by wriggling fingers where his ears should be. Concentrating hard, he shifted backwards and forwards with a series of jumps. He had overlooked how hard it was to manoeuvre the balloon on a slippery wooden floor once his head was outside, and the constant rocking was making everything swim.

Taking a small blade from his pocket, The Magnifico pierced the latex and with an enormous bang he burst free, the red balloon clutched in his left hand, as tattered as a flayed skin. Into the immediate silence, he took a deep bow. The little boy, dressed as Batman, stood up tall and proud, his black cape rippling around him, arms straight by his sides. He stared at The Magnifico through the holes in his mask.

'My daddy can do that,' he said.

Nigel didn't feel very well at all. He overbalanced and

crumpled to the ground. Distantly, as if he were listening on a badly connected telephone, he heard a small voice say, 'He could do it, couldn't he Mummy?'

Poppy detached herself from the crowd of children and adults and rushed towards him. From his position on the floor, Nigel could see the black and yellow bunting strung across the front of the stage, like twenty-one angry bees. He saw the scratches he had made in the wooden floor and a couple of balloons lying forlorn and forgotten under the table. A pair of brown brogues appeared in his eye line. Hands grabbed at the top of his arms and lifted him up.

'My wife's right, you have been drinking. Time to leave. Come on away from the children. We'll bring your stuff out. You'd better call someone to come and get you.'

'We won't be paying the other half of the fee. No point in asking.'

No doubt Sharon would have something to say about that. Nigel dusted himself down, buttoned his jacket, turned his back on the young man and walked, straight-backed, out of the hall. He stopped and pushed open the door of the men's toilet. The room was peaceful, after the noise in the hall. He wandered in and rested his forehead against the wall. It was cool against his hot skin. He heard a gurgle of water in the pipes.

His box of props was sitting in the entrance way waiting for him. Nigel felt tender towards it. As if it had been lost and somehow returned to him. The balloons shifted around as he lifted it, like pieces of a lost mosaic, thrown in without care. The box was heavy in his arms. Weighty. He must remember to collect Sharon. Through the doorway, Nigel caught sight of the boy spinning in the middle of the hall, his Batman cloak flying round him. Spinning round and round. The blue and red giraffe floated across the floor, as if it were running away.

Outside it was dark. The van looked bruised and battered, caught in the light spilling from the doorway. Nigel opened the back door and gently put the box inside amongst the burger wrappers and old newspapers. Sharon was always on at him to *clear the van out*. Shame about the Big Trick. Twenty quid down the drain. Best not to mention it before their appointment or she wouldn't be happy. He didn't want to spend an hour with Sharon and that woman *discussing it*.

He checked to see how much money he had in his wallet. Five

pounds. And some loose change in his pocket. On the way home he'd pick up a bottle of something nice for later. That might cheer her up.

Leaving the car park his headlights swept across a road sign, *Please Drive Carefully Through The Village.*

Estill Pollock

Tour of Duty

My son returns from duty incomplete
Sniper-fire declassified the cowlick
and the stammer. The honour guard's drumbeat

instructs our pace, slow... slow, but still to quick
for him to manage on his own. The flag
folds neatly to a nebula of hick

towns shining with these soldiers. If we brag,
it is as the papers note, 'died bravely.'
(A holy war presumes a body bag.)

These lost nations, compressed into TV
debriefings, seared, a theatre of war
for belt-strap bombers — Allah vis-à-vis:

the tour of duty ends along this scar
of road we follow in the mourners' car.

Derek Sellen

Othello

Paris had the temperatures of Senegal
and locusts blew through Cyprus to the mainland
while Oslo swooned. Bearing Saharan sand,
a southern wind wrapped Europe in a caul,
grains freckling our windscreen like sterile seed.
Passing famished crops in bone-hard acres,
we drove back early from the botched Shakespeare -
a blacked-up ranter, a fragile female lead -
and, itched by phantom grit, showered at home.
With Africa in our nostrils clogged by dust,
our mouths too dry to kiss, I arched and thrust.
You cried out. I could not, you could not, come.
        Later, it rained, but did not wet the core.
        A hot night. Iago dreams about the Moor.

In the Heat Haze

Connie Bott

Hi, Carolyn. How are you, child? I'm surprised to see you out on your bike so soon after your daddy's funeral. How's your poor momma doing?' The woman leaned out of her car window.

Carolyn had been walking her bike up the hill. Her hair was damp and frizzing in the heat. She was starting to feel a bit sick, but it would soon be worth it.

'Hello, Mrs. Brewster. I'm just on my way to the drugstore to get some aspirin for my momma,' she lied. She'd say anything to get out from under Mrs. Brewster's microscope. And little lies didn't count.

'You just call me if you need anything. You know you've got lots of friends and neighbours who'd be glad to help you out.'

'I'll bet,' Carol Ann thought. She was used to hints of judgement behind the sticky-sweet voices.

She started to walk again. She thought of her mother at home now, escaping into her afternoon soap operas behind drawn blinds.

'You shouldn't go out so soon,' she'd said. 'People will talk.'

'They will anyway.'

She was at the top of the hill now. She mounted the bike and pedalled hard to get up speed. The wind rushed past her. For a moment she emptied her mind and felt cool and free.

When she got home she went to the fridge, poured glasses of iced tea and took one to her mother. 'As the World Turns' was giving way to commercials.

'Did you see anyone while you were out?' her mother asked.

'Mrs. Brewster asked after you.'

'What did you say?'

'I told her you had a headache.'

Her mother threw her head back and laughed. When the commercials finished she turned her attention back to the TV.

Carolyn picked up her sweaty glass and walked to her bedroom. Her mother called out, 'If you leave your door open you'll get a draught through.' She left the door closed.

This was the worst part of the day, when the heat sapped all of your energy but wouldn't let you sleep.

She thought of all the times she'd lain on her bed, listening to her mother's laugh and her father's low angry voice coming through the wall. She tried to think back to when her parents had been happy, like they were supposed to be. She remembered a time. They were in the back yard having a BBQ the summer before last. It was something silly – the hotdogs falling into the fire and her dad trying to rescue them. They'd all laughed until they were giddy.

She tried to hang on to the memory. If she could just remember some little bit more she could hold on to that, too. She wondered if her mother ever tried to think back.

She let herself drift halfway to sleep, where her thoughts became jumbled. They stopped, as she knew they would, with the remembered harsh bang of her father's rifle coming through the wall again.

David Olsen

Wind from the Sea, 1947

i.m. Andrew Wyeth (1917-2009)

It's not much, really—just an open window
framing a commonplace Maine landscape,
easily dismissed and of no account.
Curtains of faintly patterned gauze with frayed
edges billow in the silent breath of the sea.

Wyeth's tempera palette is equally quiet
and lacking plot; context is all. Beyond
the sash of crippled Christina's attic
dormer, wheel ruts meander through
an ochre field of tawny August grass.

Between the field and a row of gloomy pines,
a stiletto blade of pewter water reflects
a barren sky. The sun, just out of view,
casts a shadow on the sill. A tattered shade
is blown askew and there's a dingy wall.

The scene is outward and within:
the boundary between refreshing space
and stagnant confinement—
the tense border of disclosure
and a veiled secret's trailing edge.

Convergence

Balanced on a fulcrum
between sleep and waking,
where identity is lost,

dexter and sinister hemispheres
converse in a language unknown
to conscious thought.

In a reverie of unreality
I feel a rocking rhythm, smell
the others' stainless sleep.

Ahead, parallels meet
and violate my faith
in geometric verities.

Silver rails converge
to an unthinkable
non-Euclidean vanishing point

beneath an iron gateway
to the new millennial truth:
ARBEIT MACHT FREI

A Leaf among Leaves

In a dim, neglected charity shop
I found a modest volume of Keats.
Wear revealed it was beloved, once.
Perhaps its owner had willed it
to heedless heirs who cast it aside,
as of no worth. The flyleaf bore,
in an immature hand, a brief
inscription: *Penelope—1913*.

Did it mark a schoolgirl's prize
or Christmas in a portentous year?
The print was clear, the paper fine.
Where "To Autumn" began, a maple leaf
was pressed while fresh enough
to bleed into the page. I imagined a girl
picking a leaf from a path through woods,
choosing this one among countless others
because it seemed the best of its kind.

She might have meandered a while,
twirling the leaf by its petiole,
and found a shaded bench or fallen log
on which to rest. There she chose
a poem to suit the season's mood
and, having read, marked her place
to arrest the time, intending to return.

The Known World

Night on the Circle Line.
A Babel of fashion statements:
hoodies, trainers and torn jeans;
or wrinkled pinstripes and shirts
with open collars and loosened ties;
others dressed beyond chic,
their individuality distilled
to conformity in nose rings
or footwear painful to see;
overdone pharaonic makeup;
improbable hairstyles
of motherless invention.

In the judder of steel wheels
over joints in steel rails,
commuters fuss with phones,
read e-books or paperbacks,
listlessly shuffle tabloids—
leaving unfinished Sudoku
or crosswords, avoiding
any glance to be answered
with a wary London Grimace.
And everywhere the weary slump
of exhaustion, the extinguished
underground night of dead eyes.

School Drills

1950s. Duck-and-cover.
At the air-raid siren's wail,
children dive under desks,
assume a foetal position;
skinny arms cover each head.
The Russians have the A-bomb
and they want to bury us.
Khrushchev said so.
We've a sworn enemy
on the other side of the world
who could strike at any time
and annihilate us all.

2010s. Lockdown.
At the bell, teachers lock
classrooms, barricade
doors, shush the kids,
and herd them into closets.
A man has an assault rifle,
machine pistol, and more
rounds than targets. Whenever
he snaps, he has the means
to kill us all. He's the patriot
in the video shop or barber chair.
He's a neighbour. The quiet one.